Inner Rhythm

Performing Arts Studies

A series of books edited by Janice Rieman, St. Louis, USA
and Christopher Bodman, London, UK

Volume 1
Music Unlimited
The Performer's Guide to New Audiences
Isabel Farrell and Kenton Mann

Volume 2
Experimental Music Notebooks
Leigh Landy

Volume 3
Inner Rhythm
Dance Training for the Deaf
Naomi Benari

Additional volumes in preparation:

Moving Notation
Jill Beck and Joseph Reiser

Nigeria's Ubakala Igbo
Judith Lynne Hanna

Making Musicians
Tony Haynes

This book is part of a series. The publisher will accept continuation orders which may be cancelled at any time and which provide for automatic billing and shipping of each title in the series upon publication. Please write for details.

Inner Rhythm

Dance Training for the Deaf

by

Naomi Benari

Routledge
Taylor & Francis Group

LONDON AND NEW YORK

First published 1995
by Harwood Academic Publishers.
Reprinted 2004
by Routledge,
2 Park Square, Milton Park, Abingdon, Oxon, OX14 4RN

Transferred to Digital Printing 2004

British Library Cataloguing in Publication Data

A catalogue record for this book is available from the British Library

Inner Rhythm: Dance Training for the Deaf.
– (Performing Arts Studies, ISSN 1068-8153;
Vol. 3)
  I. Benari, Naomi   II. Series
  792.80872

  ISBN 3-7186-5611-6 (hardcover)
  ISBN 3-7186-5612-4 (softcover)

CONTENTS

INTRODUCTION TO THE SERIES

Performing Arts Studies aims to provide stimulating resource books of both a practical and philosophical nature for teachers and students of the performing arts: music, dance, theatre, film, radio, video, oral poetry, performance art, and multi-media forms.

International and multicultural in scope and content, Performing Arts Studies seeks to represent the best and most innovative contemporary directions in performing arts education, and will focus particularly on the work of practising artists who are also involved in teaching.

JANICE RIEMAN and CHRISTOPHER BODMAN

ACKNOWLEDGEMENTS

There are many people I have to thank, for without them there would have been nothing to write. Above all, I would like to thank the children who, by trustingly putting themselves in my hands, have taught me so much and continue to do so. Also Betsy Challoner and Hildi Kappelhoff, and the many other teachers who patiently explained and told me so much when I first came to their schools knowing nothing, and who set me on the path of finding out more. I am grateful for the support of the Head Teachers who kindly allowed me into their schools year after year, often altering their timetables so that I could use their halls for classes, and repeatedly interrupting their busy schedules to come and see what the children had achieved. Colleagues, friends and relatives kindly gave their time to read through the manuscript, bringing their expertise and knowledge of education of deaf children, of music and of style, and I gratefully acknowledge their contribution. The Beethoven Fund for Deaf Children has supplied the musical instruments with which the children and I have enjoyed playing and experimenting, and I thank them profoundly for this. Lastly, I thank the charitable organizations without whose generosity this project could not have been undertaken at all: Baring Foundation, City Parochial Foundation, Chase Charity, Clothmakers' Company, Goldsmiths' Company, Hambland Foundation, Lankelly Foundation, Mercers' Company, Royal National Institute for the Deaf, Platinum Trust, and many others over the years.

LIST OF PLATES
(Between pages 34 and 35)

1. The joy of dancing
2. Exhilaration
3. Follow the leader
4. Jumping
5. The slow motion flight
6. Deep concentration
7. Watching the conductor
8. The same rhythm
9. Together
10. Watching the dancers
11. Watching the drumstick
12. Watching each other
13. His dance
14. Her dance
15. Experimenting with the tambourine
16. The letter 'p'

INTRODUCTION

I am often asked why I teach dance to the deaf.

For most of my life I was a dancer, which entails executing a number of tasks simultaneously: the dancer must listen to the accompanying music, think about what each part of the body is doing, about balance and line, the sequence of steps, the expression of a myriad of feelings in one movement, the holes to avoid on the stage, all at the same time. Not an easy matter.

Like many dancers I felt I was somehow different. I was perfectly at home with them, but in the company of non-dancers I felt inferior. I did not think analytically or linearly and could not articulate an intellectual point coherently. I could express emotion with my dance, but was aware that I also had thoughts and ideas which, although perfectly clear to me, I never conveyed verbally. Malcolm Ross edited a book about creative art which he called *The Arts: A Way of Knowing* (1983), which explored the idea that "aesthetic appraisal or apprehension is a … way of knowing". For me dance was a way of knowing.

When I first met deaf people, I realised immediately that I had an affinity with them and that their minds were very similar to mine in the way they saw the whole, and perceived space and shape. They can express a complete concept in a single sign, rather than needing a string of words in a given order, as hearing people do when they talk, and can see an object or problem in its entirety and not in pieces to be dissected. I felt close to the deaf and wanted to join their world and to learn more about it. And so I moved sideways from performing for and teaching hearing children, to concentrating on the deaf and hard of hearing.

Why Teach Dance to the Deaf?

Why teach dance to the deaf, who after all often cannot hear the accompanying music? This is a valid question, as dance and music are so intimately linked. Indeed, in some societies there is only one word for dance and music. People of these societies do not make music without dancing, nor dance without making music. In the film *Children of a Lesser God*, Sarah asks James to describe music to her. He begins to wave his arms around and then stops, saying that he cannot do so. I believe that had he continued to move, had he begun to dance, he could have made her understand its essence, for *like music, good dance has a pulse, a rhythm, a breath of its own.* If people can become aware of these and of their own rhythm, the 'Inner Rhythm', then they can dance. In fact, as the deaf use their bodies to communicate as dancers also do, it is logical to assume that the deaf can dance at least as expressively as hearing people, and probably more so.

And so my answer to those who ask me why I teach dance to the deaf is "Why not?" Almost everyone enjoys dancing and moving (Plates 1, 2). Why should the deaf be deprived of this pleasure? Dance and keep-fit enthusiasts attest to the feeling of well-being which they derive from their exercise. Movement can improve flexibility and strength. Dance also gives the possibility for self-expression, creativity, and an introduction to music, theatre and art in general. The study of dance develops skills related to other areas of learning, from simple counting to enhanced spatial awareness and understanding of shape, from an exploration of balance and equilibrium to a knowledge of weight and mass. Dance also demands and develops critical ability and self-discipline. Why should deaf children not receive these physical, mental, emotional and aesthetic benefits of dance as hearing children do?

The deaf can derive additional benefits specific to their disability: in dance, they have the opportunity to express themselves, which often relieves the frustration at having little or no verbal language with which to do so; dance can increase their knowledge of space and of their position within it; dancing with a partner or in a group can enhance their awareness of each other and their sociability in general; 'Inner Rhythm' can expand their understanding of rhythm and, with its insistence on conscious deep breathing, may in turn help the development of their speech. The acquisition of the self-discipline required for dance can be not only a most beneficial tool in other areas of life, but can also contribute to the development of a child who finds sitting still and 'academic' learning difficult.

And yet, in England, there is very little opportunity for deaf children of any age to share this experience.

Dance Provision in UK Schools for the Deaf and Hard of Hearing

Since 1970 the National Deaf Children's Society (NDCS) has been organising yearly festivals of mime. I was lucky enough to receive a grant from the Royal National Institute for the Deaf (RNID) which I used for travelling around England to visit those schools who had done well in these festivals, as well as those who were involved in the fields of dance, drama and music.

I found that very few schools indeed were teaching dance. As in the mainstream schools, the provision of the arts was haphazard, and depended on the presence in the school of a teacher with enough expertise and confidence to teach the subject.

One such school was Grove House for the Deaf in south London. The Head Teacher is a Laban-trained dance teacher, and in her school dance has always been given a very high priority. Every child has a dance session once a week, and as Christmas approaches, dance rehearsals of the Christmas show take precedence over all academic lessons. The children develop great self-confidence and self-discipline.

Another school where dance has had a high profile for many years is St John's School for the Hearing Impaired in Yorkshire. For over thirty years the children had the opportunity to learn a large variety of dance styles and techniques including ballet, contemporary dance, creative dance, tap, liturgical dance, and dances from other countries.

During the 1980s the NDCS changed the name of its annual mime festival to *Festival of Performing Arts* in order also to encompass dance. In 1993 forty schools participated in the festival. A quarter of these entered a dance number. These included movement and masks, sign song, sign rap, dance accompanying song, country dance, and movement/dance.

In 1992, dance became a compulsory subject of the National Curriculum (see appendix) in primary schools and an elective option in secondary schools in England and Wales. It was hoped that its introduction would lead to an increase of dance in schools, but unfortunately, no additional funding was made available to the schools who now control their own budgets.

In mainstream primary schools, provision of dance remains patchy. It depends on the interest of individual schools, and on their ability, and that of peripatetic dance teachers, to obtain funding. In secondary schools, where dance is not compulsory and where there are often permanent dance teachers on the staff, the number of students taking dance examinations at 'GCSE' and 'A' Level, has increased. In schools and units for the deaf, interest has grown, but the provision remains haphazard, and in some cases has actually dropped. For example, St. John's School no longer engages specialized arts teachers, and dance is no longer taught in the school.

Some organizations run occasional projects outside the schools. For example, in 1993 the Deaf Arts section of Shape London gave the first of a series of ten to thirteen-week *Deaf Dance Projects* at the Sadlers Wells Theatre.

There are a few small dance groups who work with the deaf and hard of hearing. *Common Ground Sign Dance Theatre* tours nationally and internationally, giving half-day, full-day, or two-to-three day workshops in residency, together with a performance. The members of the company teach the children "basic Sign-Dance Theatre", which is a combination of sign language and dance movement. The costs of the workshops is negotiable.

Dance For Everyone, which I founded twenty-five years ago, and under whose name I teach the deaf, tours schools and theatres giving performances of dance specially designed for audiences of deaf and hearing children. Each performance is preceded by a workshop in which the children are rehearsed in order to participate together with the dancers. The cost of the performances and workshops is borne totally by the company, who rely on donations and grants for their existence.

A few small theatre companies comprising deaf and hearing performers include movement in their work. These have been included in the appendix.

The larger dance companies make some provision for the deaf. The education department of *London Contemporary Dance Trust* offers three dance and cross-arts residencies per year for people with special needs. They do not provide classes specifically for deaf children, but these can sometimes be accommodated in their Young Place programme. The *Royal Ballet* and *English National Ballet* sometimes give workshops specifically for children who are deaf and hard of hearing.

London Disability Arts Forum campaigns for disabled people seeking to make a career in the arts, and gives advice and help to those wishing to train as artists.

Reading University offers a full-time two-year training course in Theatre of the Deaf, leading to a Diploma in Higher Education. There is a possibility that this will be extended to a third year leading to a BA degree.

This is an integrated course for deaf and hearing students wanting to work with deaf children or adults in education and community contexts. Dance as such is not included, although an emphasis is placed on "Physical Theatre, with experimentation with the visual and kinetic conditions and languages of performance". Some of the graduates perform with the *Common Ground* company.

Reading University is the only institution which provides a course of study for those wanting to work in theatre with the deaf. There is no such course for dance. To fill this gap, a charitable trust offered me, together with a deaf mime, a grant to visit schools to train classroom teachers to teach dance and mime to children who are deaf or hard of hearing. We have visited several schools and units giving half-day, full-day, and two-day workshops. We are usually also asked to include suggestions on dance in the national curriculum.

I often receive requests for information from student dance teachers who are interested in the field. I lecture and give workshops whenever I am asked to do so, and have lectured for several years on the Community Course at *London College of Dance* in Bedford.

Starting Out: Problems, Myths, Misconceptions

With further grants from various charitable organizations, I began to teach in primary and secondary schools for the prelingually profoundly deaf, as well as in partially hearing units in mainstream schools. When I first started, I believed that my only task would be to help the children learn to dance, in spite of the fact that they could not hear music, and indeed in many cases this was so. After a few months the children became aware of the relationship between dance and rhythm, and knew what was necessary to ensure that they danced rhythmically; they were fully able to integrate with classes of hearing children, taking their places proudly alongside them. However, with some children the issue was not quite so simple, and I soon found that there were many problems that had to be overcome before any teaching could take place.

The first was that not only could some children not hear the music but that most also appeared to have no awareness of the existence of the *pulse* of dance, let alone its *rhythm*, and they would dance at varying speeds, stopping to scratch and to talk as they moved. Much of my work therefore started by addressing this issue.

The second problem was that of behaviour, which can have a direct bearing on the techniques the dance teacher finds it necessary to employ. (These will be outlined in the first chapter). According to the sociologist Basil Bernstein (Wood 1988), the development of children is due in no small part to the amount of language used in their homes. Some deaf children are diagnosed late, and so do not begin to learn language of any kind until they reach school. Some parents do not learn to sign, and therefore find it difficult to communicate with their children. This lack of linguistic communication can lead to retardation of development. One outcome of this is an inability to concentrate or pay attention for even a few seconds. The dance teacher must therefore be prepared constantly to introduce new topics and demands. Some hearing children also have problems with concentration, but in a small minority of deaf children the concentration span can often be much shorter. These children will not look at the teacher's face long enough for her to finish even one sentence, making instruction almost impossible. Another result of the poverty of communication can be that parents are unable to control and discipline the children, who learn to expect the same freedom and laxity in school. Many children are understandably frustrated at not being able to communicate adequately, and some develop emotional problems. This in turn can lead to a lack of confidence and a fear of failing which, in a dance class, can show itself in the way the children are afraid to experiment and to improvise. They assume that all their difficulties arise from their deafness and so give up easily if a task appears difficult. They have not learnt the relationship between practising and success, or of trying and failing and eventually succeeding.

Language, Intellect, Memory, 'Muscle Memory', Imagination

It is generally accepted among most educationalists that the early acquisition of language is essential for the development of a child, and in our society it is assumed that this means verbal language: "In the beginning was the Word" (Saint John). The Russian psychologist L.S. Vigotsky suggested that language and communication are at the heart of intellectual development. Proponents of sign language agree that the learning of a language is essential, and argue, furthermore, that in the absence of spoken language, the acquisition of sign language is equally important in the development of young children (Wood 1988). But this language, like any other, takes a little while to learn, and in the meantime *dance* may have an important role to play. Albert Einstein wrote about the absence of language in thought, and Piaget was convinced that mental activity derives from action, and not necessarily from talk (Wood 1988). My experience, both as a dancer and in teaching dance to the deaf, has led me to agree with both Piaget and Einstein: verbal communication is not essential. Admittedly it can be harder or can take longer to put over an abstract idea without speech, but equally a whole picture can be communicated, emotions conveyed, and complete stories recounted, through sign, movement and dance. If Piaget's ideas are accepted, then it follows that dance has an enormous part to play in the education of deaf children.

Wood suggests that memory is the result of the development of the intellect. When I first toured England visiting schools for the deaf, I was warned by a Head Teacher that deaf children have a poor memory. However, in the matter of remembering movement sequences I found no evidence of this. On the contrary, at times their visual recall has been astounding. For example, a week or even several months after seeing a dance performance, many children are able not only to recount what they saw, but to dance complete sequences, reconstructing the movements, quality, dynamics and emotional content. They are also able to remember routines which they themselves have danced if the dance was adequately rehearsed and the movements were such that they required full use of the body.

Dancers talk about what they call 'muscle memory', by which they mean a state when they no longer need to make a mental effort to remember a sequence, and this occurs if movements have been repeated often. It is as if the muscles themselves remember. I wonder whether this 'muscle memory' may in part explain the good recollection of many deaf children in terms of movement, even though they may have difficulty remembering intellectual concepts. If this is the case, it might be another argument for the importance of dance teaching for deaf children.

I was also told by that same Head Teacher that deaf children have little imagination, but I found no evidence whatsoever of this. I suspect that there are several reasons why this view is held:

1. the children often have little verbal language with which to express themselves, and this is misinterpreted as being a lack of imagination;
2. much teaching of the deaf is often based on imitation, for example, signing and lip patterns have to be copied and learnt;
3. the children are often delayed in their development. Witkin (1974) talks about three stages in the creative development of children, 'Enactment', 'Iconic', and 'Symbolic'. For example, during the 'Enactment', stage, children like to 'be' rabbits. In the 'Iconic' stage, at about seven years old, they will enjoy moving 'like' rabbits. When they get to the 'Symbolic' stage, at about eleven years old, children will happily move with the quality of rabbits, imaginatively and creatively developing rabbit-like qualities into their own dances. Many deaf children are still in the literal, 'Enactment' stage, whereas, chronologically, they are expected to be in the 'Iconic' or 'Symbolic' phase.

The children's confidence in their own creativity has to be encouraged. At first, they will tend to copy the teacher's ideas. The next stage is often that of their making suggestions which are not very good or original, but if the product of these two phases is accepted and welcomed, exciting inventive work will begin to emerge, and they will begin to think about dance, to analyse and to create, long before they have the vocabulary with which to describe what they are doing.

Categories of Hearing Loss

There is a certain controversy over definitions of the varying amounts of hearing loss, and different organizations define 'Mild', 'Moderate', 'Severe' and 'Profound', according to varying criteria. However, all are agreed that a loss of over 95 decibels is 'Profound'. In other words, a child with this amount of loss can hear next to nothing. For a dance teacher these definitions are interesting but not always relevant, and for practical purposes he or she need be concerned only with three categories:

1. *Prelingually profoundly deaf* — children who have never heard and so have no memory of language or rhythm.

2. *Profoundly deaf* — children who are extremely deaf, but became so after a few months or years of life. They have a memory of sound and possibly of language, which makes teaching them easier.
3. *Partially deaf* — children who have some hearing. With the help of a hearing aid, they can hear a useful amount of sound.

1 and 2 are often referred to as 'deaf', and 3 as 'hard of hearing'. These terms have been used throughout the text.

However, all this is not as simple as it seems. Sometimes a child with very little loss has not learnt to use the hearing he or she has, and so appears to be more deaf than is the case. Other partially deaf children have scarcely any hearing, but employ the little they have, and also use their eyes to lipread and to understand what is happening around them.

Furthermore, to say that a profoundly deaf child hears *nothing* is not quite true, and this is of great significance to the teacher of dance for the deaf.

In the early days of my work with deaf children, I was greatly surprised when I found a boy (who, I was told, had absolutely no hearing at all) holding my small tape to his ear, *listening*. He was reacting, moving, not only to the low regular beat, but actually to the *music*, its tune, dynamics and volume.

My astonishment has been echoed many times by other teachers. They, too, have been surprised to observe the positive responses to musical sound — not only the vibrating-drum sound of a tambour, but also that of recorded music — by children whom they knew very well and believed to be profoundly deaf.

I have often been told by teachers that such profoundly deaf children cannot hear, but are simply feeling the vibrations. This may not be entirely true, as audiograms which are used to gauge deafness generally measure speech frequencies, whereas music can span a much wider range, employing frequencies far below and above those of speech. The extent to which ears can hear and feel vibrations can vary from child to child, as there are many causes of hearing loss and many degrees of deafness within the broad spectrum. (There is no space here to expand on this subject, but the reader desiring more detailed information on hearing loss may like to start with the bibliography at the back of this book). For the dance teacher, the fact is that most deaf children do pick up some sound through their ears or their bodies, and very much enjoy doing so. This is borne out by the fact that some will put their ears to the speakers when tapes are being played, while others will gravitate towards the sound source as they execute a given task, placing their hands or bodies on it whenever possible. This realization opened up for me a completely new and different way of using music in the dance class.

For those children who indeed cannot hear or who find it difficult to use their residual hearing, feeling the vibrations of music in different parts of the body can be of real benefit. Some derive obvious deep enjoyment from beating drums and tambours, and insist on holding the instrument as others strike it. However, contrary to common belief the feeling of vibrations is not automatic and easy. Some children can do it but cannot explain how. Others have to be made aware that they have this ability and need to be encouraged. For example, I have been told by many groups of children that they do not like tone or chime bars because they cannot hear them when they beat them, as compared with kettle drums or tambours. It can take much persuasion and experimentation until they realize that they can *feel* the very powerful vibrations. Sounds create vibrations in the air and in objects which are near the sound source. Children can be made aware of these by, for example, being asked to hold tone bars close to the chest as they beat them. As they play triangles, they can be helped to feel the vibrations in their hands and arms. If speakers or drums are put on or under the floor, the vibrations can be felt through the feet, or through the behinds as the children sit on the floor. Eventually the children can be helped to differentiate between the pitches of different sounds as they become aware of the varying vibrations they produce. It is very important that the teacher also learns how to feel the vibrations, as it is then easier to choose suitable instruments and to place them facing in appropriate directions for maximum reception of their vibrations.

Issues — Hearing and Radio Aids

The wearing of hearing aids is a matter of concern when teaching dance. Over the years they have become stronger and smaller, and many children who, years ago, would not have been able to hear very much can now do so with the help of modern aids. It is considered that radio aids which deliver sound to the ears through leads from a box worn on the chest are best for school use. With these, the voice of the teacher who speaks into a microphone about six inches from the mouth can be picked up by the wearer, regardless of their distance from each other in the classroom. In a dance class, these radio aids can have a double advantage:

1. a microphone can be placed near the music output, enabling the dancers to hear the music above the sound of feet hitting the floor, or other extraneous noises;

2. the microphone can be used by the teacher whose voice will then be clearly heard above the sound of the music or the children's feet. However, radio aids are difficult to dance in (see Plate 3): they are heavy, and unless strapped tightly can bounce up and down as the child jumps or turns upsides down, hitting the unfortunate dancer on the chin; the leads from the microphone to the aids are often long and unwieldy and little hands are often caught up in them during the execution of a large movement. The post-aural aids which have the microphone behind the ear are smaller, but they tend to fall out unless taped on, which is what professional deaf dancers sometimes do. New hearing aids are being produced which are smaller and stronger than they ever were, and I am sure that eventually they will cease to be a problem for deaf dancers.

Many children prefer to remove their aids altogether when dancing. This is often frowned upon by teaching staff who want the children to develop their residual hearing. Indeed, when working with music to which one wants the children to listen, this is not always a good idea. However, *when a lesson concentrates on developing the awareness of the rhythm of movement, the breath and the music within dance itself, hearing is not so important.*

Issues — Segregation and Mainstreaming

It was customary in England to segregate deaf children in special schools, but over the years the philosophy has been changing. Although many are still taught in these schools, a growing number are now placed in units which are integrated into the mainstream for most of their lessons. An advantage of this, suggested by the research of Alec Webster and John Ellwood (1985), is that language development is enhanced by interaction with hearing peers. On the other hand, deaf children often feel themselves to be inferior and do not mix with their hearing classmates as much as expected; when learning dance together with hearing children they will often automatically assume that the hearing are better than they are, and will tend to copy them rather than take the initiative for themselves. I therefore prefer to start teaching deaf children by themselves, and only later when confidence is established, to teach them together with their hearing friends.

Even when being taught alone, the children often give up if they anticipate that they will not be able to execute what is asked of them, and they play about rather than risk failing. The obvious answer to this is to make the tasks basic and achievable, although the danger of this is that if they are *too* easy, the children soon become bored. The demands made on them have to be challenging but possible, and this needs constant vigilance and the ability to modify requests at a moment's notice.

If other hearing adults are in the room, it is a good idea to ask them to join in so that the children can see them try and sometimes fail. This helps the children become aware of the relationship between trying and practising and ultimately succeeding. Many children often do not realize that by repeating an attempt they can improve their performance.

Where children are integrated, it is essential that the children who are deaf or hard of hearing receive enough support in the classroom, in the form of an interpreter constantly to explain everything the teacher says. If they do not have this, and they do not understand what is happening, they stop concentrating, and it is very hard to persuade them to pay attention, as they have acquired the habit of letting their eyes wander as they daydream. The problem is compounded in a dance class which happens in a larger space where it is possible to face in many directions and where self-control is essential, where the children share space and therefore have to be aware of each other, where creativity can only happen when there is enough self-discipline to allow freedom of thought and action, and where interaction is also an important ingredient.

Issue — Age

Some teachers prefer to teach children only after they reach the age of eleven or twelve, when they have already acquired some degree of self-discipline and physical ability. However, my firm belief, grown out of long experience, is that *dance training is most effective if started with the very young*, as soon as they start school or even before. In this way they become aware of the demands put upon them, of the use of space, of relating to each other, and above all of the fact that dance can be fun. At first all tasks are set in the form of games, but gradually rhythmic and physical demands are increased, and by the time they reach the age of eleven or twelve they are capable of far more than if they were only just starting.

I find it is necessary constantly to reassess the children's emotional development and ability to execute a given task, and to resist the temptation to assume potential according to chronological age. In this book I will describe how I modify and develop each task as the children's competence increases, always keeping an open mind and being ready to change my requests immediately if I see that the children are more or less developed than I had anticipated. For older pupils and adults, the same principles apply, and possible ideas will, I am sure, suggest themselves to the teacher and the older students as they work together.

Although the teaching of many skills starts with definite demands on my part, this is only to give confidence and to initiate the process; my aim, once good communication has been established, is to allow the students' own creativity to take over as soon as possible, enabling them eventually to devise their own warm-up exercises, set their own rhythmic tasks and create their own dances.

This book will cover many facets of dance teaching, encompassing physical training, developing awareness of self and space, creativity and aesthetic growth through self-appraisal and analysis. These areas are all included in the *National Curriculum for Dance* (see appendix), and indeed form part of the dance curriculum in most vocational schools. Specific attention will be paid in the book to the development of rhythmic awareness.

Although primarily about dance, simple ways of teaching music have also been outlined. The close affinity between dance and music has made it impossible for me to teach one without relating to the other.

Examples are given in every section, not with the intention that they be used as described, but rather as a starting point for teachers and their students who can go on to create more relevant ideas and themes for themselves. Sometimes subjects are referred to more than once because they fall into a variety of categories.

It is hoped that these pages will be of interest not only to trained teachers of the deaf who would like to know more about dance, but also to dance teachers and therapists who feel they need more knowledge about the deaf and hard of hearing. I hope that both groups will forgive the outlining of what to them may be already obvious.

This book is a chronicle of my personal search for ways in which to help children who are deaf and hard of hearing to benefit from and enjoy dance as much as their hearing peers, and as such is a work-in-progress: the children never cease to teach and inform me.

1

COMMUNICATION

Teachers with Children

The question arises: How does the dance teacher communicate with the children? The obvious answer is "body language", the mode of communication we have in common. This is indeed true for most of the time, as very often much can be taught by simply demonstrating. But there are occasions when there is a need to evoke an image which will stimulate the children's own ideas. In such cases demonstration would defeat the object: they would simply copy.

When teaching hearing children it is often possible to create a picture with words, or to obtain a desired dance quality by modifying the volume and tone of voice, or choice of words. Action songs, nursery rhymes and poetry can be employed, but these are not easy options when working with the deaf. In addition, simple instructions like "again", "stop", "now" have to be imparted constantly, and so the need for another common language becomes apparent.

To Sign or Not to Sign

In schools where the children sign, signing is an obvious solution. However, this is not as simple as it sounds, for there are many views on this. Most signing schools in England will teach "Sign Supporting English" (SSE) in which key words are signed, or "signed English", in which every word is signed and where the order of the English language is adhered to so that the children will learn the language of the country in which they live, its grammar and its rules. However, many deaf adults, who cannot hear the spoken language, and who therefore do not need to follow its order and rules, advocate the use of British Sign Language (BSL). They say that its grammar, order and logic best reflects their culture. It is more natural for deaf people, and deaf children will often use it or a variation of it, when communicating with each other, particularly if they belong to deaf families. But the use of BSL by a visiting teacher in a school which employs SSE may raise a few eyebrows, and may not be too popular with the staff.

The same issues arise in many countries. The deaf population of France use French Sign Language (FSL) and deaf Americans communicate in American Sign Language (ASL). Hearing teachers in their schools often prefer to use a system in which all words are signed in the order they occur in the spoken language.

Equally, in a school which uses the aural method of communication because its staff believes that signing will retard the development of speech, the use of signing may be very well-received by the children, but cause the staff to throw up their arms in horror declaring "They will never learn to speak!" I suggest that the visiting dance teachers clarify these issues before starting work.

Most schools now favour "total communication", a combination of sign and aural methods, and whichever language is used in a school, the lip patterns are of utmost importance, for it is these which the deaf person watches — whether depending on them totally if no signing is used, or to aid understanding if it is. All words must be articulated clearly but without exaggerated lip patterns, and it is therefore necessary to ensure that the face is always clearly lit. It is extraordinary how may times it happens that after dancing round in a circle with the children, or moving round the hall amongst them, one stops to talk to them and finds oneself with the back to the window, the face in shadow, where nothing can be seen at all!

Focusing Attention

Another important side of communication is, of course, reception. Many deaf children find it difficult to understand their hearing teachers for a variety of reasons. One explanation which applies to all deaf people is that unlike hearing which happens whether one wants to listen or not — *watching*, hearing through their eyes, or "seeing voices" as Oliver Sacks (1990) called it, takes an effort of will, a definite decision, to look and to receive. Whether a child is only lip reading, or is relying on lip patterns as well as signs, this receptive action can be taxing, and needs real concentration.

In addition, in a school hall or large classroom where there is the possibility of running around and facing in many directions, it is necessary to devise ways of focusing the many pairs of eyes on the teacher before communication can take place. Most deaf people have a wonderful sense of fun, and a good way to establish communication and to impart any message to deaf children is through a game. With every group I meet, I start the session for the first 6 or 7 times with a

"Watch Me" game. (In fact every task set thereafter is accomplished more successfully if presented in an entertaining way.)

At first, the only aim of this "Watch Me" game is to focus the children's eyes on the teacher. The children dance around until the teacher signs "stop". In this way no sound is involved and all must use their eyes to the same degree, however much or little hearing they have. If the teacher and children like the idea of competition, the last one to stop can be "out". The game can later be modified to watching a drumstick. The teacher beats the drum and when the drumming stops the children must also stop. Here those with a little hearing are at an advantage, and can turn away as they dance, knowing they will be able to hear when the drumming stops. As lessons develop, the game becomes more sophisticated. It becomes possible to drum slowly and fast, strongly and weakly, with pauses, and finally to introduce definite rhythms which must be reflected in the dancing.

Another game for establishing communication is "Follow-the-Leader". The children follow the teacher and later each other round the hall copying the leader's movements. Again, this can become more complex as they develop their physical and rhythmic skills (Plate 3). Observation of the children initiating movements for others to follow can be very revealing and useful for the teacher who can learn much from noting the quality of movement. For example, a child-leader's movements may be aggressive, expressing anger, or repetitive and similar to that of others, showing possible lack of confidence and creativity. Sometimes, children selected to be leader do not dance, but mime such feelings as sadness or fear.

Watching colleagues is an essential part of any group dancing, one which all professional dancers have to master. Deaf children also need to develop this skill. When practising a dance for a performance, I will insist on this towards the end of rehearsals. However, too much reliance on watching others has specific disadvantages with deaf children. The more profoundly deaf a child is, the more he or she will usually tend to watch and follow those with more hearing, will do everything 'late' and will not develop a real sense of rhythm. As mentioned above, it is for this reason that it is best to work with children who are deaf and hard of hearing on their own until confidence is established, before integrating them with their hearing peers.

Some teachers in vocational dance studios are unduly wary of having deaf children in their classes, even when this stage has been reached, and the children have acquired confidence and a rhythmic sense in prior dance training. These teachers should be assured that communication *is* possible: a child who is committed enough to want to attend a ballet class, for example, will watch the teacher carefully when he or she speaks. It is important for the dance teacher to make sure that the lips can clearly be seen. Actually, this is often easier in a dance studio than in other situations, for even if the teacher has turned away from the student, the face can usually be seen in the mirror.

Wherever possible it is preferable for the dance teacher to use the means of communication employed by the deaf, and there are a number of accepted and effective ways in which this is done. The teacher can select each as appropriate in any given circumstance. For example, one method to attract attention is to wave the arms, but in a dance class this may not be effective as the children may at any time be facing in different directions as they dance, or may misinterpret this as an example of how to move. Another way is to bang or stamp on the floor, but again this can be ineffective as much banging and stamping go on as part of the dance activity. Alternatively the lights can be flashed on and off. The deaf often initiate communication with each other by touch, and when deaf and hearing work together, the hearing ones often touch their deaf colleagues to give them information about starting a dance, standing still, or changing direction etc.

Dancers and Sound Sources

It is important to place the children near the sound source, so that they will find it easier to hear and to feel the vibrations. In a ballet class, a piano can be held instead of a barre so that the vibrations can be felt directly. If taped music is used, it is useful to place the speakers on the floor and, where possible, to ask the children to remove their shoes and socks, so that the vibration are more easily transmitted, and also to boost the bass as the majority of children will have more hearing loss in the higher frequencies. However this is not always the case: a profoundly deaf girl reacted to no music at all until a recording of a flute was played. To everyone's surprise, she was able to dance to this accompaniment, following not only the tempi and pauses, but even the high and low notes in the tune.

It is of course preferable, where possible, to use live music rather than recorded music — the vibrations of all instruments are much easier for the children to feel. Tambours and kettle drums have strong, low vibrations, and those of the piano are also fairly easy to feel. Teachers should experiment with and learn to play a large variety of instruments, as different children will respond to different sounds and vibrations, and will constantly surprise their teachers.

Music with a loud low beat — for example, some types of African and Caribbean music — is usually suitable, but it should not be assumed that this is the only type of music that can be heard by the deaf. As illustrated above, the children will respond to a wide variety of musical stimuli, depending on the degree and area of their impairment.

Some teachers find it difficult to choose and obtain suitable music and recordings for their dance classes. I have found many helpful people in music libraries and record shops where simply saying "I am looking for some music for a dance about space, or fish" will produce many useful suggestions. There is no quick solution to this problem. I suggest listening to music whenever and wherever possible, with a pen and paper handy to note names of suitable choices. (See appendix for a list of pieces of music which I have found useful for specific activities). In the next chapter I discuss the advantages of teaching dance *without* music.

Dancers and Space — Spatial Awareness

The spatial awareness of profoundly deaf children sometimes develops more slowly than in hearing children, and seven and eight year-olds often tend to use space as if they were several years younger, standing and moving in close proximity. The result of this can be bumps followed by tears, and the children have to be helped to become aware of space, floor patterns, and their place in this. By dancing in circles, straight lines, diagonal lines and other shapes, and by increasing awareness of their own bodies, they gradually become more confident and able to dance in their own space without trespassing on that of others.

Dancers and Others Dancers — Socialization

As already mentioned in the introduction, children who are profoundly deaf may be retarded in their social development. Also, their peripheral vision may be under-developed as a consequence of their intense concentration on watching lips. Both factors contribute to children having problems relating to others as they dance. While they may develop real body awareness, and may execute difficult technical feats, they often do not watch each other. Games need to be devised which will develop this ability.

Simple exercises such as "mirroring" can be introduced: two children stand facing each other with hands touching; one child moves the hands, arms and whole body while the other child copies the movements. This can later evolve to the execution of movements without touching and the introduction of a variety of directions, rhythms and dynamics. Similarly the children can stand one behind the other, shadowing, or they can collaborate in making a variety of shapes with their bodies.

The folk dances of many countries give wonderful opportunities for dancing together and watching each other. Many dances are performed in circle formation which gives a feeling of community, and most of these dances have basic rhythms, and steps which can be further simplified if necessary. Children usually love repetition as this inspires confidence, and they are happy to repeat the same sequences over and over again. English Country Dancing and square dance as well as Israeli, Greek, Arab, Indian and Sri Lankan dances are often very suitable. (See Chapter 6 for detailed descriptions of an English and Arabic folk dance I have used successfully). In England, West Indian dancing is also very popular although not necessarily danced in circles or pairs, as the music usually has a regular loud low beat and the movements are familiar, being similar to what children can see on television.

The teacher must take care to give a strong indication to the children as to when to start dancing. Although the beat can often be heard or felt, the melody usually cannot. A hearing person can usually tell from the tune where they are within a phrase, but it may all sound the same to a profoundly deaf person. On one occasion a group of secondary school children were performing a pop dance which they had choreographed, and although they watched each other, counted and danced rhythmically, they started two counts too late, with the result that the whole dance was executed out of time with the phrasing of the music.

Although many musical choreographers prefer the dancers to feel the breath and the phrasing of the music and to express it in their dance, many professional dancers count as they dance. This can be very inhibitive, particularly for children. However, I have found that many deaf children insist on counting as they move, as if they enjoy the physical sensation of doing so. At first I tried to stop them, but then I saw their fingers appear as they counted in sign. I realised that deaf children resort to this physical "counting" because they cannot count the rhythm silently, (or "rehearse" the rhythm in their heads) as hearing people do when they dance.

Piaget describes the way hearing children repeat words internally as they learn to read as "rehearsal" (Wood 1988). But deaf children cannot do this, as they have no sound memory which can remind them of the sound of the words. Equally, in dance, they have no sound memory to remind them of the counting numbers, or of the rhythm of the dance itself. Nor do they have sound-symbols for remembering the steps or moves of a dance. When a hearing person learns a tap dance, for example, he or she will repeat: "shuffle, *hop*, (pause), step, tap ball change".

To overcome this problem — which is compounded by the fact that deaf children often have no awareness of the existence of pulse or rhythm — I began to devise a method which I called "Inner Rhythm".

2

INNER RHYTHM

Breathing

In my search for a way to inculcate an understanding of dance, I started from the premise that if deaf children could not hear the music and had no knowledge of the regularity of pulse, or of the variations of rhythm possible in dance, *I had to help them become aware of the rhythm which is in the body*, and from there of the rhythm, dynamics, breath and phrasing which is in every dance movement.

We all have a heartbeat and a pulse which can be felt and danced to. We have our own *inner rhythm*, which is determined by our metabolism and our mood, and which can be varied by the speed of breathing. For example, if one breathes slowly one can slow down the rate of the heartbeat.

I started by suggesting to a group of children that they feel their pulse and then try to walk at the same speed. However, they all found it very difficult to find and feel it. I then asked them to breathe deeply but found that many could not do so. Many profoundly deaf children "devoice" when speaking, that is, they mouth the words but do not make sounds and so have no need to breathe more than shallowly. I tried various tasks employed by speech therapists, such as games in which the children were required to race dried peas which they blew through a straw, or to keep a balloon in the air, but to little avail. Then one child suggested that it would be easier to feel the pulse if they were tired out, so I asked them to run around until they were exhausted. This led to a real breakthrough, as I discovered that there was now no reason to feel the pulse: if they ran until they dropped, they breathed deeply, even those who had never done so before. I now began to devise dances which required large movements and deep breathing, and the children executed these beautifully and rhythmically. However, I encountered an unforeseen problem in performances: when people get nervous they tend to breathe rapidly and more shallowly. On many occasions a dance had been well rehearsed, but at the performance the dancers breathed faster and so moved hurriedly, often losing the pulse and the quality of the movement. When a dance involved large movements throughout, this problem did not arise to such a degree, but even in these, nerves often caused the dancers to breathe faster, making their movements smaller and less well-defined.

My experience as a dancer had taught me that when dancing energetically with others, as when folk dancing, one finds that all begin to breathe at the same speed: the tempo of the dance has determined the rate of breathing. I wondered whether this could happen in reverse: if dancers were encouraged to breathe at the same tempo, would it be easier for them to dance in time with each other?

Conscious breathing is an integral part of the training of many professional dancers, both ballet and contemporary. An inhalation can help to sustain a balance or a slow movement and can ensure that a jump is high and stops in the air at its peak; an exhalation renews energy and prepares for the next breath in. It can also help achieve a smooth fall or roll. However, deep breathing is not an easy request to make of children who usually do not want to be bothered with something so intangible.

One solution is to ensure that every dance has sections in it requiring large movements and therefore deep breathing, and to insist that the movements remain wide and extended. This often leads to the making of involuntary sounds, particularly with very young children. (Incidentally, these can be encouraged as a tool in speech training, as it is easier to make sounds when executing strong movements than when sitting still). Another way to encourage the children to breathe deeply is to show how this would enable them to execute a technical feat more easily. For example, a slow motion action replay or a dance on the moon require slow sustained movements, which can more easily be controlled if the breathing is deep and slow.

I realized that breathing could be a very useful tool in helping children become aware of the existence of rhythm and of their own inner rhythm. I felt that if they could acquire this awareness, they could approach dance *in silence* in the same way as hearing people, moving on to an understanding of the rhythm and breath of their dances. Speech therapists were interested in my ideas, as one of the problems the deaf and hard of hearing encounter when learning to speak is the rhythmic element. They were also engaged by the possibility of enhancing the use of the voice through rhythmic and strong movements. Since then some teachers of the deaf have become convinced that these methods are successful for the development of speech.

Silence

The idea of dancing in silence is not a new one. Marie Rambert (1972) advocated it many times throughout her life; Doris Humphrey and Jerome Robbins both choreographed ballets without accompaniment; and now the proponents of New Dance often do so, stating that they are more interested in the rhythm and the breath of the movement itself than in subjugating it to the music.

There are many advantages of dancing with children in silence. One is that recorded music, performed with adults in mind, is often too slow for children; they have shorter legs and faster heartbeat and move more quickly than adults. Apparent unmusicality in both deaf and hearing children is often simply a physical mismatch.

A specific benefit of working in silence with deaf children is that those with more impairment will not feel inferior to those with more hearing, and will not try to follow them. In professional companies of deaf and hearing dancers, the hearing dancers are often required to lead the deaf, turning the deaf dancers in effect into second-class citizens. For educational purposes I feel it is better to confront the whole class with the same situation.

Many schools for the deaf sometimes put on performances in which the children are accompanied by fluid music without a definite beat. This may increase the pleasure of the audience, but is of less benefit to the children.

I like to conduct a class in silence, develop the feeling of the pulse and an understanding of the rhythm of the dance. Only then I may sometimes add music with a loud beat, or I may even beat the rhythm which the feet make as they dance, — in the way that Indian dance teachers accompany their pupils, — to remind them of each step.

Émile Jacques-Dalcroze

I realized that my work had many similarities with the thinking of Émile Jacques-Dalcroze (1921), and that I was incorporating some of his ideas. He was a music teacher of hearing children in Germany and Switzerland at the beginning of this century. He noticed that when people sang they were inclined to speed up or slow down according to their temperament or mood, but when they sang and marched simultaneously, they kept perfect time. He held, in common with dancers, that the muscular system perceives rhythm. He believed that every child possesses a sense of time, and that because rhythm is essentially physical, muscular memory is achieved by the repetition of dynamic physical exercises. Then, according to Dalcroze, a child is able to hear without the help of the physical ear. He was of course referring to hearing children.

One example from my experience illustrates the strength of "muscle memory" and its relationship to rhythm. I remember working on a dance in silence with a profoundly deaf girl. We returned to it about three months later because I wanted to incorporate it into a longer work, this time to pre-recorded music. She remembered every move of the dance, but it was impossible to get her to dance in time with the music she could not hear. Her muscles remembered having danced the dance at a slightly faster tempo.

Incidentally, I discovered that one of Jacques-Dalcroze's findings was relevant in the case of deaf children. He had observed that when children played or sang they often were not in tempo, but that when they *walked* at the same as playing or singing, they *were*. With deaf children, I discovered that walking was not energetic enough to help them feel and maintain the tempo when playing an instrument. But when I introduced large movements involving the whole body, the results were truly exciting. As described below, I later explored this combination of dancing and playing in a variety of ways.

Every class or workshop I give now starts with a very energetic warm-up section in which large movements, particularly of the torso, are used; this initiates deep breathing, and it is then easier to obtain rhythmic motion.

3

THE WORKSHOP OR CLASS

With the central purpose of fostering the "Inner Rhythm" of each child, it is useful for the dance teacher to start by setting out the aims (long term and more immediate) of a workshop or class, and to prepare lesson plans stating how these will be approached. Of course, one must be ready to modify these targets constantly, as the time span will vary from class to class and from child to child. It is therefore advisable to keep a regular note of each child's progress in the different activities, and to work at the pace of each class; to set tasks in such a way that each child in the group can execute them at his or her own pace and in his or her own way.

The aims of dance workshops and classes are many:

1. To increase awareness of the body;
2. To strengthen it, to help it become pliable and supple;
3. To develop physical skills: jumping, turning, balance, travelling;
4. To extend awareness of line, shape and space;
5. To enhance the ability to interact socially and to cooperate with others in small and large groups;
6. To encourage a sense and understanding of rhythm and breathing, tempo and dynamics, a feeling for music itself; to develop the "Inner rhythm";
7. To nurture an analytic ability and true creativity;
8. To encourage the use of dance to communicate emotions, feelings, actions, and story;
9. To enhance the self confidence of the children and to help them develop an alternative language with which to express themselves;
10. To develop the self-discipline necessary to achieve all the above.

As I stated earlier each class consists of many varying sections in order to keep the children's interest. A constant component of almost every section is the rhythmic element, with the exercises and tasks being set to a regular pulse, so that gradually an inner awareness of this pulse develops. This growing inner awareness of pulse prepares the child for the introduction of varying rhythms, and is the root of a full-grown "inner rhythm".

Warm-Ups and Exercises

Wherever possible I like to stand in a circle with the children, so that all can see each other. This also engenders a feeling of communality.

I usually start with a warm-up which stretches or tones each part of the body in turn, starting either with the feet and working upwards, or with the head and working downwards. This follows the same format every time, as the children's confidence is enhanced by executing movements with which they are familiar. However, it allows for small variations and development so that skills continue to grow and body coordination to develop. (Occasionally a child will at first object strongly to changes, wanting to repeat the exercises exactly as he or she remembers them, and leading me and the class into the next sequence after the prescribed number of repetitions).

The type of movements chosen can vary, and can be drawn from keep-fit, jazz, modern or classical dance, or any other discipline, as long as they do not make any unnatural demands on the body.

It is often necessary to devise special exercises for the knees. If the knees are locked, rhythmic moving of the body is almost impossible. A sequence of simple knee bends can be set, made more interesting as the children are asked to add different body and arm movements, directions and later walks or steps.

Self-awareness grows through the execution of full movements. For example, when asking children to raise the arms, I urge them to involve the whole body in the upwards stretch. Confidence is also enhanced. It is as if it is only when the dancer feels the *whole* body that he or she is able to move into it. This ability to extend every action to the utmost is also important in developing "muscle memory". As discussed in the introduction, this "muscle memory" is an important tool for the deaf, who have little sound memory or ability to let the music remind them of a sequence in the way that hearing dancers do.

Many small children prefer to have a reason to move. If they are asked to imagine that they are reaching for a ball or an apple, they will stretch higher than if requested to simply "lengthen a muscle".

Alternatively, very young children can be asked to shake different parts of the body, at first copying, but later having their own ideas, and being allowed to shake their ears or hair or anything else they consider appropriate or funny.

When confidence and familiarity are established, children of all ages enjoy making circles or other shapes with different parts of the body, and thinking of how many they can find. If done with enough energy, this too can be a very satisfactory warm-up.

As body awareness, strength and general technical ability progress, so satisfaction grows and creativity is enhanced.

Tempo Awareness

If the children come into the hall in an obviously excited frame of mind, or if the theme for the session is to involve sustained movements, the whole-warm up exercise period can be executed in slow motion. This calms the children and prepares the way for them to choreograph their own slow sequences. Moving slowly also has the advantage that it helps awareness of the movement itself, its direction, shape, quality, and so on.

A popular theme using slow motion movements is a "visit to the moon". If the children are old enough the effect of zero gravity can be discussed; if they are younger, they can be shown films. If this is not possible, they can simply be told that they would move very slowly in this situation. This is a good opportunity to introduce deep breathing as it is not easy to move slowly, and deep inhalations facilitate the sustaining of slow movements. Rhythmic structure will develop which can then be discussed and incorporated into the task as they dance in silence. If preferred, one child can accompany the others on the drum or tambour, or alternatively set the tempo and rhythm which the other children must follow.

A slow motion ball game like an "action replay" can stimulate much interest and many lively ideas. Possible movements can first be explored by standing in a wide circle and slowly throwing an imaginary ball to the next person. This is then developed by hurling the ball high and making the recipient jump for it; rolling it low, requiring a bend down to catch it; or flinging it far to the side, necessitating a long reach for it. Finally, the movement of catching is continued, usually developing into a turn which leads into a throw. It is now possible to improvise a game of netball, dividing into two teams, and making a rule, for example, that the ball is kept by each team for two throws before being intercepted on the third. A regular beat can be provided which accompanies each propulsion, and to which the other players also move, swaying as they watch the ball, building up a dance with a pulse and rhythm of its own, one which comes from the movement itself.

A slow section with deep breathing at the end of the session will often help to calm the children down and be ready to resume their academic work. This will be welcomed by the class teacher!

Dynamic Awareness

Deaf children sometimes find it hard to understand the concepts of "strong" and "weak", often confusing these with "slow" and "fast". Drumming cannot help in this case, as weak or quiet drumbeats cannot usually be heard. I have found it useful to set a section of only weak movements, followed by one which consists only of strong energetic ones. It is then possible to conduct a whole session consisting of movements which are executed both strongly and weakly, with and without energy, to help the children appreciate the difference between varying dynamics.

The development of this awareness can take time, and I like to include in almost every workshop a section on impetus, on swinging arms or legs strongly and energetically which result in moving other parts of the body. For example, swinging the arms round the body can result in spinning on one foot, jumping round with the legs underneath or with the legs flying up in front or behind; swinging the arms sideways can lead to sideways jumps, or leaning sideways, or being suspended to the side on one leg; swinging the arms upwards can greatly enhance the height of jumps; swinging forward will increase the amount of forward movement. The request to swing an arm or leg and to "see what happens" can lead to much enjoyment as well as pride and confidence as children evolve their own movements which are different from anyone else's.

A development of this is to set, and later to request, rhythms involving accented and weaker movements, in which the strong dynamic moves can instigate turns, jumps, travelling, while the weaker ones do not.

I have discovered that the use of music notation also reinforces children's understanding of the concepts of "strong" and "weak" (see Chapter 5).

As children often like to have an expressive, dramatic or emotional reason for moving in one way or another, a popular theme which most can relate to is that of creeping quietly in fear of a monster and then meeting such a frightening creature or giant who stamps loudly making strong movements. A dialogue can be created, allowing interesting rhythms to emerge, comprising slow and fast, strong and weak movements and sounds, as well as pauses, as one child creeps away, and is then followed by his or her monster. As well as developing awareness of rhythm and dynamics, this situation necessitated the children looking at each other and being aware of each other's actions.

Some children very much enjoy moving energetically and aggressively, and it is obvious that they are releasing pent-up frustration and anger. Very quiet, shy or withdrawn children, on the other hand, often resist exhibiting this quality. It is interesting to see how gentle insistence on this can result in a form of release for them also, as they realise that they too can dance with conviction. This can have a positive effect on their activities outside the dance class, as they gradually learn to assert themselves and to interact in a more assured way with their classmates.

Although this could be described as "dance therapy", therapy is not the main aim of this work but only a side benefit, as indeed it is of dance in general. Deafness is rarely an alterable state, and teaching dance to the deaf is, in itself, not dance therapy.

Travelling: Jumping

All the above tasks can be executed travelling round the room, or across it diagonally in turns, giving the opportunity for the use of strong dynamics and covering a great deal of space without the danger of bumping into anyone else. In addition, many children enjoy the chance to be seen dancing alone.

As in any professional class, jumps are developed slowly, first giving small movements of the ankles, pressing the toes into the ground to warm the feet, then setting small jumps with both feet, and then from foot to foot, then turning while jumping, travelling across the room, adding impetus from a swung arm or leg (Plate 4).

Deep Breathing

It cannot be stated often enough that it is important to include in each workshop or class a section where the children need to breathe deeply so that they learn to dance in a sustained or controlled way. All activities which enhance breathing and which link breathing strongly with movement contribute to the growth of "Inner Rhythm" in the child. One source of inspiration for such activity is the subject of "the sea", which offers a plethora of moods and movements, from calm and peaceful to stormy and violent. The children usually come up with many beautiful ideas, particularly for a rough sea. When these have all been explored and experimented with, suggestions can be made on how to create a wave by falling forwards in the way the water throws itself to the ground; this could also be executed by falling to the side or backwards; a sweep from standing could also be done from kneeling. It is then possible to work in pairs and then in groups, creating a sequence of waves.

It is here that inhalation and exhalation become important, as the waves begin to move in harmony or in sequence one after the other. Deep breathing can help ensure that the waves rise and fall in relation to each other without the need for the children to watch each other constantly.

Another fertile idea is that of "mermaids", which I introduced once to group of twelve-year-old girls. We discussed the quality of movement which results if dancing under water, and they explored the possibilities of dancing without legs, or rather, in their case, with both legs stuck together, and made up an inventive dance. It contained a few moves from "breakdance" which was popular at that time. I found that this caused some problems, as the more able ones could execute these with more ease and speed than the less-talented. However, when deep breathing was introduced and they understood how this could help them accomplish the moves, the results were beautiful. As mentioned earlier, it is vital that deaf dancers learn to maintain their deep breathing in "performance conditions" if they are to preserve the tempo and quality of movement they have acquired in rehearsals. In this case, the use of video was helpful in demonstrating this to the dancers. I had proudly decided to video the performance of the mermaid dance. As has happened so many times before and since, I was disappointed with the result. On the videotape the girls appeared nervous and embarrassed and looked as if they wanted to get out of the limelight as soon as possible; they breathed fast because of their nerves and moved as hurriedly as they could, never finishing a single movement. It was not until the girls saw the video that they became convinced of the importance of coordinated deep breathing. I have learnt that the only way to overcome the problem is constantly to insist on controlled breathing.

Another activity which involves deep breathing is "being balloons". It is easier to sustain a light, floating quality with full lungs after an inhalation, exhaling as the balloon descends, only to rise again on the next inhalation. This theme is surprisingly popular with children of all ages.

Cooperation and Imagination

True cooperation can only occur when the children are confident and secure. Therefore I find that it is often a good idea to begin any new activity with a task — whether it is a rhythmic exercise or a creative choreographic one — which allows each child to execute something successfully alone. Then one can ask the children to collaborate in pairs, and later in large groups.

Imaginative dance based on a theme such as the "Visit to the Moon" (already discussed in the section on "Tempo Awareness") can have several phases which lead to a high degree of cooperation between children, while stimulating creativity and nurturing awareness of shape. It could also be expanded into a creative choreographic project which could be developed over a whole term.

Continuing with the idea of a "moon visit", let me illustrate they way that individual creative tasks can lead on to cooperative ones in several phases. One might begin by suggesting that the children imagine themselves as space travellers to the moon or another planet. Next one could suggest that the space travellers find strangely-shaped rocks on the moon, and ask the children to "become" a different rock or stone. This is then developed as the pupils are asked to get into pairs, and then into groups of three to create larger formations. Very young children may have to be stimulated at first by drawings of different stones.

The children can then be divided into two groups, one being the space travellers, and the other the rocks. This second group might then be asked to form different shapes, making sure that the rocks they make have holes in them that space travellers can crawl through. The travellers are then asked to walk on the moon. On encountering a rock, they are to go round it, over it, or through it, (always moving in slow motion to obviate the risk of injury).

It could then be suggested that on the moon there live some strangely-shaped creatures; some are round, some are square, some have only one leg, some none at all and so have to find an alternative method of getting around. The children are asked to create these and other creatures, and later to move according to their shape: to hop, to bounce, to roll. The same request is then made of pairs or groups of three.

Once an integrated class of deaf and hearing participating in this activity was asked to find as many different shapes as possible. On this occasion each pair comprised either deaf or hearing children.

There were no mixed pairs. It was interesting to note that the deaf children reached a far higher number of shapes because they communicated physically, moving each other into position. Whereas the hearing ones told each other first what they wanted and then executed it.

Another note about cooperation: in a mixed age or ability class, wonderful results can be obtained by mixing the more able with the less so, as they will tend patiently to help and explain to their slower friends, at a more appropriate level of communication and use of concept than the hearing teacher can often achieve. This is an activity which benefits not only the less able child, but also the more competent one, who consolidates his or her understanding by the act of instruction.

Dance into Drama

In the "Visit to the Moon" activity, children usually let their imagination determine abstract shapes as requested, but sometimes their work takes on a more dramatic aspect: for example, when the stones acquire the shapes of humans frozen in an tableau depicting a specific event. Equally a request for a demonstration of strange creatures encountered on the moon can sometimes develop into a dramatic mimed dialogue as the space person and creature meet each other, rather than the expected exploration of varying shapes and sizes of space monster.

The degree of dramatic involvement in what was originally set as an abstract task depends on the emotional maturity of the children as well as on on their personal preference. Sometimes a dramatic theme can be a more stimulating starting point for a dance workshop for young children, who may find it easier to mime real events or actions. Mime is, of course, a totally valid art form and there is a place for it in education: it requires attention to minute detail of position, movement and placement, and because of its affinity in this respect with sign language has particular significance for the deaf. But it must be remembered that it has a language and a discipline of its own which is different from that of sign and also from dance. In general, one could say that dance stresses more line, rhythm and overall flow of movement.

Shaping Actions into Dance

In a dance class focusing on creativity, it is necessary for the teacher to first accept children's natural mime-like actions where these occur, and then to help them to turn these movements into dance. This is sometimes a difficult hurdle for the inexperienced teacher, who often rejects everyday movements and gestures because of uncertainty as to how to tackle the problem. There are several ways the teacher may help dancers shape their movement ideas:

1. By enlarging the naturalistic movement, even to the point of stylization, until the whole body is involved. For example, when digging, to bend the whole torso forward and bring it upright again, rather than letting the arms alone execute the movement;

2. By introducing repetition of movement;

3. By becoming aware of the rhythm which results from the repetition;

4. By executing the movements in pairs or in groups, executing the same movements on different levels, at varying speeds, in canon, in a variety of floor patterns;

5. By exploring the mood and feelings of a "character", and representing the character by body shape. For example, a sad person may drop his or her chest and drag the feet, executing every action from this basic position, whereas a happy confident individual may have a lifted torso, hold the head high and have a bouncy step.

Creativity

Much has been written about the creative process and there is no need to elaborate on this issue here. In my experience deaf children are as wonderfully creative as hearing children, in both an exploratory, "stream of consciousness" approach, as well as a more cerebral, analytical method, once they have the confidence to feel that they can be. Lack of confidence can show itself initially in an apparent reluctance to think about and create movements. This is only a temporary phase, which can be overcome by the teacher suggesting a task or theme and then herself or himself putting forward and demonstrating some ideas. This can be done when requesting the creation of rhythms, or movements to a given rhythm, and also when dealing with themes involving the creation of atmosphere, mood, actions or stories.

For example, on one occasion I asked for circles with different parts of the body. On receiving no response, I demonstrated, saying: "You could do it like this, or like this, or like that. Now you think of some more circles". The children copied my suggestions exactly: one little girl even remonstrating with the others because they had not repeated them in the same order. Only later did they think of their own new ideas. I feel that the children have to be given a vocabulary before they begin to develop one of their own. I found myself giving very formal set lessons at first; it then became possible to ask for movement ideas and to suggest the execution of them in different directions: forward, backwards, sideways, turning, or at different levels. (Varying movement qualities also come automatically with the understanding of dynamics introduced through rhythm and music). Soon it becomes possible to start every task with my ideas and then to go on to those of the children. Their ideas tend at first to be not very original, but gradually become more expressive and truly interesting if enough time and patience is given for the less creative period to be worked through. Eventually examples from the teacher do not have to initiate a project, as the children's own creations take over and replace them.

My example of "making circles" above suggests an avenue for creativity which differs from that inspired by theme, story, mood or character. Deaf children, like hearing children, can enjoy dance for its own sake. Different aspects of it can be explored purely from the point of view of movement itself. There are many possible ways to motivate original, personal ways of moving. For example:

1. To set a move such as an arm swing to the side, and to ask the students "to see where it takes you". It could lead the body in the direction of the swing, instigating runs which lead to a drop to the floor, a roll which takes the body upwards into a standing position again, and so on;

2. The drawing of curves in space by the body could lead it to making further circles or other shapes;

3. A change of weight can initiate a wide variety of movements depending on which way it is transferred;

4. The execution of movements repeated with different qualities can lead to interesting results. Props could be used to initiate some of these as, for example, watching the way silk scarves float as they are thrown or flicked into the air;

5. Changing the tension from one limb to another can lead the body in untold directions;

6. Two people together can explore what happens as they pull away from each other, gradually varying the tension, or transferring from one to the other; they can see what happens as they lean on each other, slowly gaining confidence as they trust their weight to the other person.

Sequences

Once the children have become adept at improvising and creating their own movements, it becomes possible to develop their ideas and to structure them, to put together short dance sequences. If a strong image can be evoked — whether it is abstract or theme-related — that image itself will begin to instigate sequences as confidence grows.

It can be hard to remember what was created in this explora-tory, creative state of mind, and a useful tool is a video which can record and later play back what was created. (This differs, of course, from the use of video mentioned earlier to help create and give feed-back on dancing in performance conditions. Here one uses video the way an artist a sketchbook, or musicians a tape recorder). Another way is for the teacher to observe carefully and to remind the pupils verbally or by showing them. Another excellent method is to ask the children to perform their own movement in turn, and then to teach it to three or four others, who then dance all the movements in se-quence. Having children teach their own dance movement has several advantages: it ensures that the task will be within the capabilities of most of the other children; it gives an opportunity for the young "teacher" to really think about and analyse the movement as he or she watches the rest of the class, correcting it as necessary; it enhances the "teacher's" confidence.

Dancing all the sections in sequence can be difficult; the obvi-ous answer is repetition until the "muscle memory" takes over. This can be successful if turned into a game so that it does not become bor-ing. For example, each child may take it in turn to lead the others.

"I went to market" is another game I use for creating a se-quence: I ask one child to show his or her ideas and all learn it; then we add the suggestion of another child and perform the two consecu-tively; then a third's contribution is learnt, and the three parts per-formed. This is repeated until all the children's creations have been in-corporated.

The teacher can guide this process, so that the movement ideas can be added in a suitable order, in varying directions, and with ap-propriate repetitions, until a well-built dance is constructed. It is help-ful to introduce a rhythmic structure, for example by linking the move-ments of two children together, executing them alternately, or the first three times and the second once.

Once this stage has been reached it is possible to go on to putting together longer and longer sequences until complete dances can be created. Gradually the issue of construction and form can be introduced, as one does with hearing students. The children themselves become involved in the larger creative process, discussing the criteria and making decisions about form and structure.

Process and Product

When setting a physical task, a rhythmic exercise or a creative session, it is important for the teacher to evaluate the relative value of process and product at any given time. Sometimes the children will gain most from simply thinking about and producing movements and rhythms. At other times some children may rightly be very proud of what they have done and want to show their friends, while others may feel insecure and would prefer not to be looked at. Children who have not done very well may be stimulated by seeing the work of their classmates and will ask for an opportunity to try again. When the children are encouraged to watch each other in a positive, rather than a critical way, feelings of insecurity will diminish. All the children will gradually learn to analyse movement, as they see one child executing a sequence well or creating an interesting movement, and another failing. If a video camera is used, they can also learn to assess their own work, which can spur them on to greater achievements.

Performance

Sometimes the children are encouraged to work hard by the thought that at the end there will be a performance for the whole school or for their parents. Again, the teacher must weigh carefully whether or not to set such a goal. While creative sessions can be fun, and showing the results of the creative process can enhance confidence and pride, the rehearsal over and over again of what has been done until it is good enough to show to an audience can be tedious and boring, and involves quite different abilities and new skills. Performing for an audience requires more awareness of what colleagues are doing so that movements can be coordinated, the building of dances which have dramatic cohesion, the use of a performing area with entrances and exits happening at prearranged times. On the other hand, the self-discipline needed for a public performance is a most useful attribute for any child, and the pride at achievement can be very great indeed.

The choosing of a subject or image which will inspire the youngsters to want to work on a performance can be daunting, but need not be if the teacher is in tune with his or her pupils. Possible themes will be outlined in the following chapter.

4

CREATIVE DANCE: THEMES

As already discussed, there are times when a teacher feels that his or her students are better motivated by having some theme or dramatic stimulus rather than by exploring dance "for its own sake". This chapter is a resource for those occasions. The number of themes on which to base such a creative session or to build a performance is boundless, limited only by the imagination of the teacher.

Inspiration can often be found in relating the dance workshop to the work of the class teacher. This approach is often favoured by class teachers, since it can reinforce ideas and vocabulary being introduced in the general classroom.

With very young children whose language and signing is limited, the use of pictures is often a very direct way of stimulating them and of imparting the subject matter, and sometimes the introduction of implements and tools can also be particularly helpful.

Noah's Ark

A class of five-year-olds was learning the story of Noah's Ark with their class teacher, and we decided to make a dance about it. The children knew that Noah had made the ark, but when asked how he did this were completely blank, and simply pointed to the picture of the ark. When I suggested that he made it out of trees some of the children were upset and denied this hotly. It was only when real saws, hammers and nails were brought into the hall and each child was given a chance to work with them, that they understood the idea and we were able to go forward.

As we enacted the story of building the Ark in dance, I encourage the children to enlarge every natural movement so that they could become aware of what they were doing and also to enable them to move rhythmically. They marched into the forest with their "pretend" tools over their shoulders. They stood in a circle and sawed until they watched the trees fall down. Then they took imaginary hammers and nails and banged, their bodies going lower as the nails went in. Gradually the rhythmic element became apparent as I beat the tambour while following their movements. When the ark was finished the children became animals, and jumped in two by two, each pair moving in the way typical of their chosen creature.

Older children in another group were able to devise their own movements for the construction of the ark. One class decided to use saws which required two of them to operate it together, and much fun was had trying to coordinate their actions with the imaginary tool. They found out for themselves that the only way to do so was to move rhythmically, making big movements with their torsos. These movements followed the swing of their arms and showed clearly which way they were going at any given moment. A third child was then asked to accompany them on the tambour, following their rhythm, but at the same time helping them to coordinate their movements.

Balloons

A real object was also useful in stimulating movements on this theme. When I asked children of varying ages to "be balloons", all thoroughly enjoyed being blown up and popped. But when asked to drift and float around, the running of most of the younger ones bore little resemblance to the quality of a floating balloon. However, when a real balloon was brought into the hall and the children watched it for a moment, they quickly adapted their movements. As I mentioned in Chapter 3, a useful aid to achieving this quality is the conscious use of breathing, inhaling while floating and exhaling as the balloon lands. This deep breathing will in turn lead to a regular pulse as the dance determines the rhythm.

Water

As mentioned in the last chapter, themes of "the sea" and "waves" offer many possibilities for inspiring movements which can develop conscious breathing, and can be a source of constant invention.

Underwater Creatures

A favourite subject for younger children is the creatures who live in the seas. Older children also enjoy this; once they have exhausted the possibilities of crawling around on their stomachs "being" fish, they often start moving in the way characteristic of sharks and jellyfish, exploring different movement qualities, as well as floor and group patterns.

Mermaids

I have already described the dance activity by twelve-year-olds on this theme. I also introduced the idea of "mermaids" to a group of seven-to-eight-year-olds. To stimulate creative thinking, I asked them how they would move with a tail instead of legs. When I explained what mermaids were, children asked if they really existed. I said that although they did not, they do occur in story books, and the way was cleared for some wonderfully inventive ideas. At first the children simply crawled on their stomachs and later hopped with both feet together, but gradually they began to find more ways of moving about, rolling flat and then on their knees and revolving on their knees and behinds. I then suggested that they pretend to play ball, and invention started to flow, as the children flung their bodies around in their effort to throw and catch the imaginary ball. This led to their working out how they would execute other games and everyday activities, how they would fall and pick themselves up, and finally how they would dance. As they moved the dance itself created its own rhythm, its own breath, and accompaniment was not necessary.

Seaside

"The seaside" offers a variety of possibilities for building dances, apart from depicting the sea itself: paddling, swimming, jumping waves, looking for sea shells and crabs, (or being crabs), building sand castles, putting on suntan lotion, exercising and sun bathing. All offer opportunities for creative thinking, dancing in unison, and interesting rhythms which the children can devise and execute to accompany the action.

Rain

"Rain" is another theme which has yielded a lot of fun and has stimulated much imagination. Raindrops slowly dropping or rolling down the window pane, heavy storms, playing in the rain, jumping in and out of and over puddles, splashing each other, trying to keep dry under umbrellas. A recording of "Singing in the Rain" with its strong repetitive rhythm can provide a very suitable accompaniment to which the children can be asked to make up a dance. Awareness of each other has to be stressed in an effort to avoid any accidents with the umbrellas!

Wind

The "Rain" theme can lead to an exploration of different weather conditions and how humans react to them. "Being" the wind can necessitate blowing, a very useful accomplishment for the deaf, as well as providing an experience of powerful movements of the arms, torso or legs, as the wind controls everything in its path. Children can imagine being blown by the wind, being pushed forward, sideways, backwards and in circles; discovering the difference between deciding to move in a certain way, and being moved by an outside force; exploring what happens when the body moves away from the perpendicular, gaining confidence and courage as they realise that this gives many possibilities for wonderful movement as they play with weight. Ultimately an off-balance position can lead to a fall, and this in itself offers great scope for exploration and the building of a technique which enables the body to reach the floor without injury.

The children can be asked to work in pairs, one child being the wind, the other being blown by it. The wind can initiate the movement, blowing the head which causes the other child to lean or fall; or the feet can be blown which makes them move away from under the centre of balance; the wind can blow from behind or in front of the body, or can cause it to revolve as it blows around. This activity is good for enhancing an awareness of others, their movement quality, direction, speed and phrasing.

Snow and Ice

Cold can lead to snow, the shape of a snow flake, the way the snow falls, and activities in the snow, such as making a snowman or woman, throwing and dodging snowballs, or being hit by them, building up a pulse or rhythm as they are thrown or avoided. Snow suggests ice, the shape of icicles, the way in which Jack Frost might move as he makes the ice, or by contrast, the smooth sailing quality of ice skating.

A more cerebral creative process can sometimes be employed for example, by initiating a discussion on what to do if feeling cold; it can lead to talk about circulation and its relationship to movement, and an exploration of the actions which might result from trying to keep warm. Whole dances can be built up from arm swings and stamping feet, again necessitating an awareness of each other.

The effect of temperature on the way we move can be discussed and explored, and this can lead to a deeper understanding of tempo, as an activity or dance can be speeded up as the participants endeavour to keep warm, or slowed down as the sun shines more strongly and the heat increases. This can also tie in with classroom lessons on temperatures in different parts of the world.

A story which utilises wind and sun is the Aesop fable, *The Sun and the North Wind* (1993), and there is a charming West Indian story *Anansi and the Weather King* which lends itself to a look at many weather conditions and their effects on humans and animals. Many of the folk-tales about Anansi (1990) make a wonderful starting point for work on this theme.

Animals

Young children (and sometimes older ones) find animals a constant source of inspiration and pleasure. They seem never to tire of "being" jumping rabbits or frogs, slow heavy elephants, giraffes, or galloping horses, executing exactly the movement qualities of each animal. The rhythmic element can easily be expanded and developed by suggesting that children pause as the animals stop in fear or to eat, or to pounce on their prey.

Older pupils may want to explore the dance quality, say, of a tiger waking up and stretching slowly, stalking his prey, and pouncing on it. This can evolve into pairs working opposite each other or in groups, dancing in varying relations, floor patterns and sequences.

Clowns

Clowns are usually popular with children, and their varied activities can be executed combining humour with rhythm; they walk along a tightrope carefully and slowly, then confidently and fast, setting up interesting rhythms as they do so; they march into the ring and fall over at regular or irregular intervals; they can turn around in different directions, dodging or bumping into each other, necessitating close cooperation; or they can throw custard pies, causing their adversary to fall over, all breathing *in* deeply as they prepare to throw and *out* as they do so, breathing *in* as they await the missile, and *out* as they land on the floor.

Festivals

Relating the theme of dance sessions to a topical event or festival can be most productive, as it ties in with the children's home life and often also with other aspects of the school's activities. For example, Guy Fawkes Day is celebrated with fireworks in England as is independence Day in the USA, and much fun can be had exploring the varying ways the rockets, Catherine wheels, golden rain, move as they shoot into the sky and drift to the ground in a myriad of shapes and colours. This can be developed into group dances, as the fireworks are let off in unison or in sequence, from different positions on the floor. They can take off at different speeds and in varying relations to each other, in different rhythmic sequences, which can be accompanied on musical instruments by other children.

Emotions

Emotions are a broad area which can be explored through movement and developed into dance. This can start with a discussion on what happens to the body while experiencing different feelings. For example, when a person is sad the feet feel heavy, the shoulders tend to slump and the head to drop. When frightened, eyes dart around and the feet move carefully.

The children can be asked to walk while expressing these feelings. A set dance routine can then be executed, and the ways in which it would be modified in terms of tempo, dynamics and body shape according to the emotion being portrayed can be discussed. Eventually the dancers can make up their own sequences to express given feelings, alone or in groups. Once this area has been explored, it can be incorporated into dance dramas.

Dance Dramas

The children's liking for dramatic depiction can be utilised in the creation of dance dramas. Sources for the dramas may be in stories which the children know, or subjects with which the teachers wish to familiarize them. Dance dramas also give opportunities for work in other areas of the curriculum, such as art or creative design, when the children themselves plan and make their own sets and props.

Religious or cultural festivals are a constant rich source of material, as the relevant stories, myths and legends can be turned into dance dramas. These can be constructed rather in the manner of an opera, with dances to establish the characters and to describe their mood, interspersed with sections based on mime or enlarged from natural actions and/or signs, which advance the story. Each character, his or her age and mood, can be discussed and an appropriate position or shape can be established for each one before going on to explore how each would move in any given circumstance.

Improvisation can play a large part in this, as the children first dance or act out their own ideas. The teacher can then select the most suitable parts, or eventually the children themselves can watch each other, analysing and deciding communally which part of the improvisations to use, and in what order, so as to create well-structured viable dances.

The Christmas story gives opportunities for older children to explore a tired dance by Joseph and Mary, and for dances for shepherds, kings and angels. The younger ones can execute dances of sheep and other animals which the children consider were present in the manger.

The Hindu Diwali story also easily lends itself to dance drama comprising: a dance of the deer which Sita sees in the forest; a sad and lonely dance by Sita when she is left alone in the forest; a careful hunting dance as Rama stalks the deer; an aggressive dance by Ravana the ten-headed monster and his followers; a dance by the monkeys as they happily build a path of stepping stones across the sea, which Rama then crosses as he goes to rescue Sita; and finally a joyful dance with lights, as everyone celebrates her return.

The use of festivals and folk tales of many cultures offers additional advantages:

1. The festive and folk music of many African and West Indian countries, for example, often has a strong percussive beat, which deaf people in particular can find stimulating and can be helped to reproduce;

2. The opportunity to learn about other cultures can sometimes be easily and pleasantly initiated through the study and performing of their stories, using as far as possible their dance style and their music;

3. In schools where there is a wide cultural mix, this can aid understanding between the members of the different cultures, going some way to help break down prejudice which so often is based on ignorance;

4. It can give children from the ethnic minorities a deep sense of pride that their teacher and their whole class are learning about and dancing stories from their culture.

Folk and Fairy Tales

Folk and fairy tales and legends with which most children are familiar are also a rich source. For example, the Gingerbread Man gives an opportunity to think about shape, about how a biscuit or cookie in the shape of a man would move. He is not soft so cannot bend his knees or run in the ordinary way. Once one or two suggestions are made as to how he could propel himself, children usually come up with many more: he can jump, hop, spin 180° on each step, he can sway from side to side, and always the rhythmic element can be used, the teacher setting up the rhythm, or the children accompanying each other. In addition, the cooking actions of the Old Woman and Old Man can be made into a dance, or left as mime, and of course the animals who chase the Gingerbread Man are a vehicle for discussion and imitation of movement qualities and speeds, as well as being a source of great pleasure.

For young children, the *Three Little Pigs* (1978) gives opportunities for three work activities, as the pigs each build their house. The children can first discuss how a house of straw, wood or bricks is made, breaking down the activity into several sequences. For example, straw is collected, tied into bundles, and these are then piled on top of each other. For the house of wood, trees are chopped, wood is sawed, nails are hammered in. For the house of bricks, mortar is mixed, a layer is set out, bricks laid on it, more mortar is spread on the bricks, and so on; windows and doors are put in, and finally the roof is placed on top. All these work activities lend themselves to rhythmic structure. The wolf walks or runs to each house, and the dialogue which includes "I'll huff and I'll puff and I'll blow your house down" can be either signed or spoken or both, according to the priorities of the class teacher and the school. The chase where the wolf tries to catch the pigs is always greatly enjoyed.

Older children are often inspired by heroes of their favourite TV programme, "Superman" and "Teenage Mutant Ninja Turtles" being recent examples. It can be very healthy for both teacher and children if the children have to bring these characters — perhaps unfamiliar to the teacher — to life through dance.

Some older children prefer to make up their own stories and to devise their own themes, and this can be an opportunity for the teacher to introduce questions of composition of movement and music, (or choice of music if the children have some hearing), movement quality, use of space, development, structure, — in fact, everything which goes to make up a dance.

Work Activities

As with the house building of the *Three Little Pigs* or the sawing to build the Ark, many work activities are a good starting point for dance, as they usually have a built-in pulse and rhythm: for example, digging, vacuuming, or cleaning windows, have an obvious pulse; other activities such as cooking, planting or weeding can be executed in a rhythmic way.

Robots

Robots hold a fascination for many youngsters, and are a useful vehicle for reinforcing the concept of strong, dynamic, rhythmic movements. The strong pulse of the work activities above can be exaggerated, allowing the movements to be executed in a robotic fashion. Almost any activity can be done in a mechanical way, and one child or a group of children can beat a pulse or a more complicated rhythm to ensure evenness of tempo and uniformity.

Sport

Most sports also have a strong rhythmic component and so lend themselves to be made into dances, for example: golf, cricket, baseball, tennis and table tennis, with their rhythmic swing. The repeating of each movement, identically or with variations, keeping the movements small, or enlarging them to encompass the whole body, are all good starting points for dance.

As described in the previous chapter, a game of catch played slow-motion allows for an exploration of the movements, shapes and levels involved in throwing and catching a ball, and again, the movement will itself develop its own breath and phrasing.

Fight

The idea of slow-motion can also be used for fight sequences. Divide the children into pairs and make three rules: there is to be no physical contact whatsoever, they must take it in turn to initiate an attack, and every movement must be followed through and be carried on to the next. That is, if A hits the left side of B's chin, B will be turned to the right and as the turn is completed he or she will hit or kick A, who in turn will react, finishing his or her reaction with an attack on B. These slow large movements will necessitate and should produce deep breaths which in turn will result in the dance having its own pulse and rhythm stemming from the movement itself, needing no accompaniment. The fact that this exercise is executed in slow motion ensures that no injury should occur, and that the children become aware of each other's movements and of the dance itself, as well as developing an understanding of line and shape (Plate 5).

Shape

The lines and resulting shapes which the body adopts when executing this stylised slow-motion fighting can be discussed and examined. But shape can be explored in its own right before being used to express or depict feelings or activities. For example, the letters of the alphabet, first alone and then in pairs or groups of three, are great fun and are a useful starting point, before going on to flowers, houses with doors, mechanical instruments, machinery, icicles, etc., which can change shape, melting into other patterns on a given sound. This can be done either by talking and signing, or alternatively, by manipulating the limbs of others (Plate 16).

Giant Signs

Many signs used by the deaf to communicate are very evocative of what they depict. Enlarging these to involve not only the hands, but the arms and whole body can be a wonderful starting point for dance. For example, the English sign for fire, in which the hands imitate flickering flames, can start small and low as the dancers crouch on the floor, gradually growing as the performers stretch up reaching to full height. The flame can bend and weave, and then sparks can dart around the hall (with a bit of poetic license!). The flames can be part of one big fire as all the participants cooperate, making a circle or travelling like a bush fire, growing at the same time, or taking over from each other.

Pop Dance

Another constant source of interest for older children is pop dancing. Most children want to be able to do it, if only because they need to conform. They have seen it on TV and usually have an immediate understanding of the style. For these reasons it is a good starting point for dance if working with older pupils who have not had much dance training. An added advantage is that there is usually a loud low beat, and the rhythm is usually even, consisting of simple eight-count phrases with little if any variation. However, one pitfall can be the fact, as mentioned above, that recorded music is played by adults and for adults, and can be found to be too slow for children, particularly if they cannot hear very well.

The children themselves can often remember several dance movements they have seen, and a dance can be built up repeating each one eight times. It can be helpful to beat the pulse on a drum or tambour, or to beat only the first of every eight counts, or any other rhythm found to be suitable.

After this has been achieved, it is relatively easy to move on to pop dances of other eras. For example, Rock 'n' Roll has a distinctive rhythm which can be drummed and danced. The style can be explored, and videos can be shown to inspire the youngsters into experimenting with some of the lifts, choosing whatever they feel they can execute, and later devising some of their own.

Other popular dances from this century lend themselves easily to being developed in a dance class. For example, the Charleston, Tango, Twist and Hand Jive, can all lead to a curiosity about dances of other times: the Minuet, La Volta, Polka, Waltz, Foxtrot, etc., with discussions about the mores and clothes of each period which produced these dance forms, as well as enquiry into their tempo, meter, dynamics and rhythm.

Plate 1   The Joy of Dancing

Plate 2 Exhiliaration

Plate 3 Follow The Leader

Plate 4 Jumping

Plate 5 The Slow Motion Fight

Plate 6 Deep Concentration

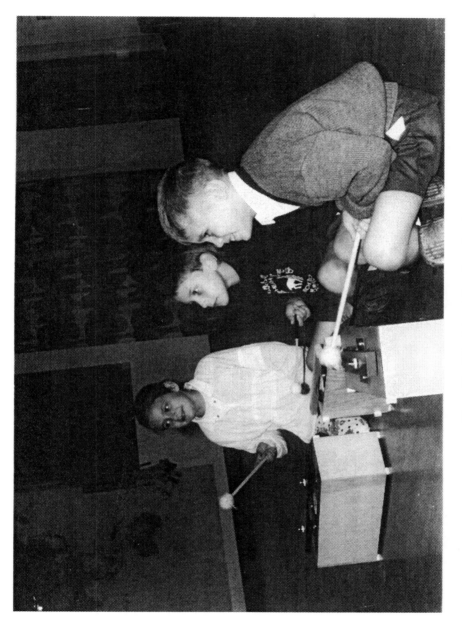

Plate 7 Watching The Conductor

Plate 8 The Same Rhythm

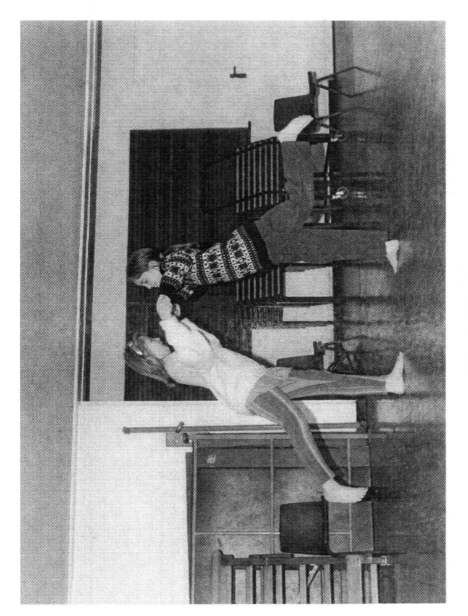

Plate 9 Together

Plate 10 Watching The Dancers

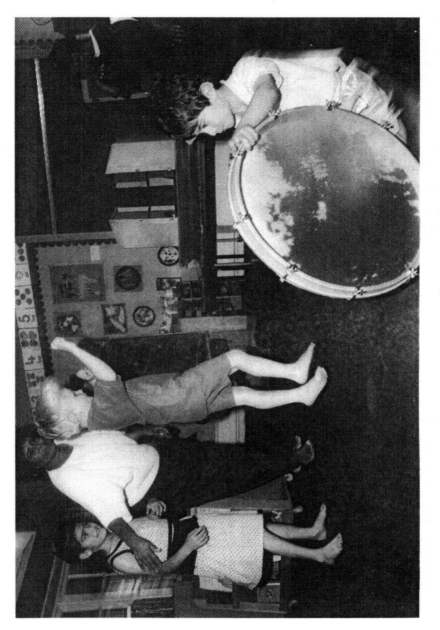

Plate 11 Watching The Drumstick

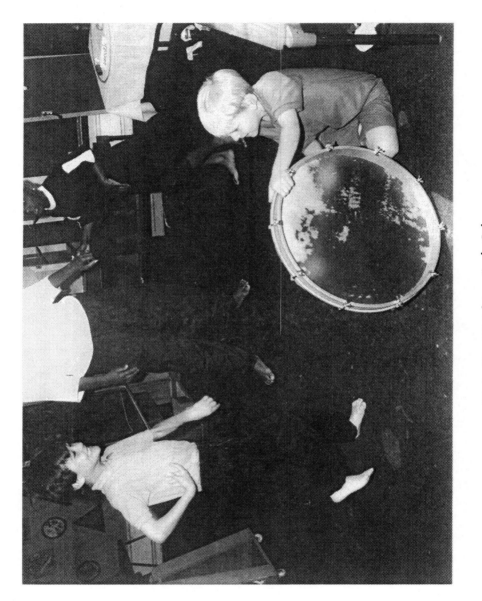

Plate 12   Watching Each Other

Plate 13   His Dance

Plate 14   Her Dance

Plate 15   Experimenting With The Tambourine

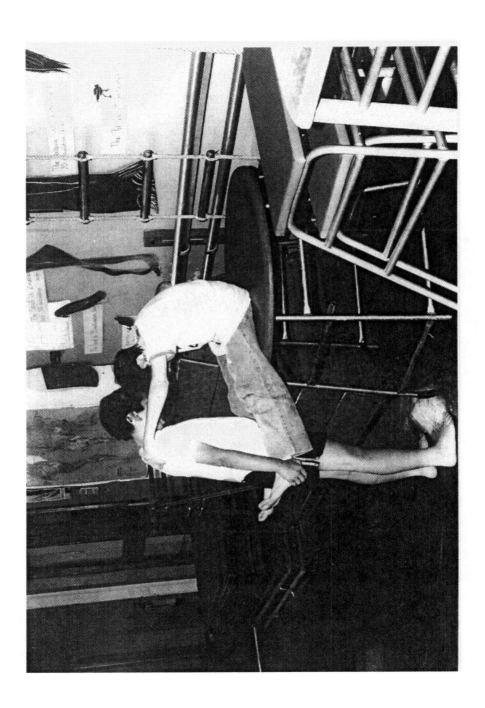

5

PULSE AND RHYTHM

Rhythmic Exercise

As rhythm is such an integral part of dance, I try to enhance understanding and experience of it in every part of a class or workshop except sometimes the creative session. As discussed in the chapter on the class or workshop, warm-up exercises are always undertaken in a rhythmic way, allocating the same number of counts to each exercise before moving on to the next, but leaving one or two counts at the end of each section to allow for the children to realize that a different movement is coming. For example, "six upwards stretches, hold two counts, six arm swings from side to side, hold two counts".

Alternatively, it is possible to execute each action strongly or weakly, putting these two qualities together in varying ways. For example, a swing with the arm can be done twice strongly and then twice weakly, or once strongly and three times weakly; an exercise can be practised at different speeds as, for example, a shoulder rotating twice slowly and four times fast. If a dance with a more complicated rhythm is to be taught later in the session, its rhythm can be used throughout the warm-up section to familiarize the children with it; for example, two slow and three fast.

Each exercise can be done in this rhythm.

Travelling across the floor can continue the theme of a simple rhythm, different tempi or dynamics: for example, two slow runs and three jumps from side to side. The same rhythm can then be employed in the creative section of the class, where the children can be asked to work alone or in pairs, thinking of as many ways as possible to dance to the same phrase, using different parts of the body, in different directions and on different levels (Plate 8, 9).

A simpler sequence can be used with three to five-year-olds. For example:

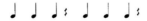

Three stretches upwards and a hold, each repeated four times, followed by three shakes of the hands over the head, and three near the floor; three shakes of the hips, three knee bends, all repeated four times. This can be followed by jumps in sets of three, in different directions, on the spot, turning or travelling. When the children are tired, they can sit and drum the rhythm on the tambour, and then can get up and think of different ways of dancing the same rhythm.

Folk Dances

When this rhythm "in four" is firmly established, a dance can be taught. For example, here is a version of a simple English country dance or square dance I have used successfully with deaf children:

The children stand in two lines and do four skips towards each other and four back. Initially some will skip four times and then take one count to change direction, delaying the start of the backward skips by one count. This can be remedied by asking them to execute not four but three skips in each direction, allowing one count for their change of direction and weight.

An additional section can be added: seven skips and a pause, and the two can then be joined together:

They can now now skip round each other and back to their places, taking eight counts. Three to five-year-olds may not be able to count up to seven, but will still be able to skip in and out and then skip round each other rhythmically, the rhythm and pulse having been established on the skips in and out. The children usually very much enjoy the next part of the dance in which the two lines skip round outside, the leaders meet and form an arch which the other children then skip through. The whole dance can then recommence with another pair at the top of the lines. Additional sections can be put in according to the dancers' ability, as for example letting the pair who made the arch gallop up and down the centre while the others stand and clap, dosi-dos, swing-your-partner, the Grand Chain, or any other variation thought of by the children or the teacher.

For seven to eight-year-olds a slightly more complicated rhythm can be attempted:

first by clapping or drumming, then by making up little dances alone or together. A different ending can then be added: ♩ ♩ ♩ ♩

after playing the

♩ ♩ ♫ ♩

three times, making

♩ ♩ ♫ ♩ | ♩ ♩ ♫ ♩ | ♩ ♩ ♫ ♩ | ♩ ♩ ♩ ♩

Finally a simple version of an Arab "Debka" can be taught, using the same rhythmic phrase throughout:

1. Standing in a line holding hands, following each other: two slow runs, three fast, three times, and then four even runs round self. Finish standing next to each other;

2. Step forward R, hop on R, three steps back, all three times, and then four steps round self;

3. With hands behind the back: walk to right, starting on right foot, two slow and three fast, finishing with the weight on the right foot and the left toe up, heel on the ground; repeat this to the left and again to the right, and finish with four steps round self;

4. Join hands again, and follow each other: two slow runs, and three jumps on the spot turning a quarter turn to left, to right, to left. Repeat three times, followed by four runs round self.

Older students may prefer a disco dance. They can beat the rhythm, learn the appropriate footwork, and then accompany each other.

Clapping

It can sometimes be easier to communicate a complicated rhythm by asking the children to sit and clap it before trying to dance it, and if large movements are used and the arms and whole torso are involved, the pulse and rhythm can quickly be experienced and understood. For example, children can sit cross-legged on the floor and beat alternate hands on the floor at the sides of the body, leaning far to the side on each contact. This use of large movements helps to establish an even beat, which does not necessarily occur if small gestures only are employed. For a rhythm comprising varying divisions of the beat, the slow ones can be executed by hitting the floor at the side far away, while faster ones can be clapped or banged on the floor in front of the body, emphasising the contrast in a spatial way. This also makes it easier to remember the sequence.

Drumming

In the introduction to this book, I spoke of my discovery of the great pleasure the profoundly deaf children derived from playing drums and tambours, obviously hearing or feeling the strong vibrations. I wondered whether it might be possible to work from this end, from the making of sounds, to the enhancing of their understanding of rhythm and music in the same way as for hearing children — in other words to work *from* drumming, *from* the hearing or feeling of vibration, *to* dancing, *to* "Inner Rhythm", *to* dancing itself.

Equipped with simple tambours, (of the Orff type used by music teachers) and soft-headed mallets, I began to experiment. At first, as I asked children to drum, definite rhythms were not discussed. By simply requesting "a few" slow beats, or "lots of" fast ones, the concept of varying tempi was introduced. Gradually I included requests for specific numbers of fast or slow, pauses or accented beats.

I found it helpful to set different sized movements for different speeds. For example, for the quarter note or crotchet, ♩ a large down-up movement of the arm; for an eighth or quaver, ♪, a smaller movement; for a rest, ₹, a sideways movement of the same size as the beat, while nodding or rocking the body. I have found that deaf children often execute this movement while signing and saying "nothing", and I now always introduce the concept of the rest or pause with the word "nothing". Alternatively, hitting the other hand instead of the instrument is also effective.

When drumming a rhythmic phrase, it can be helpful to beat different parts of the drum, making a visual pattern which helps in remembering the sequence.

I have seen both this idea of visual pattern on the drum and that of different-sized movements for different tempi and dynamics used to wonderful effect by an orchestra of taiko drummers, consisting of about twelve Japanese (hearing) children playing kettle drums in Hyde Park in the autumn of 1991. The whole piece had obviously been very carefully choreographed, incorporating large arm and body movements, jumps, stepping back from the drums and running towards them and so on — all resulting in perfect musical unison while the players executed very complex rhythms.

When a child cannot understand a rhythm, it is often helpful to tap it into his or her hand, or better still onto the upper chest, so that it can be felt. An even more effective way, when in a dance class, is to move with the child, holding him or her very close so that he or she can feel the movement of the teacher, but this is not always appropriate, as some children can get embarrassed. Alternatively, the teacher's rhythm can often be transmitted simply by holding hands with the child. The teacher gently pulls the child in appropriate directions and exaggerates the bounce as he or she moves, establishing the connection between movement and beat. The use of tone bars to reinforce this understanding can have advantages:

1. Because tone bars are specially made to produce large vibrations which are felt in the body, the children can learn to feel these, holding them close to the body as they play;

2. Large numbers of tone bars are easier on the ear of the hearing teacher (and others nearby!) than a whole class of drums.

The next stage will be for the children to play instruments together. A "Conductor" game helps to foster the ability of the children to relate to each other as they play, and to watch a conductor. It is played as follows: the teacher — later a child — points randomly at different children who then beat once, twice or three times as directed. The teacher imperceptibly modifies the randomness until she points at each child along the line, and the children are asked to play in turn without being pointed at, thus developing awareness of each other's playing.

The game is then extended by asking the children to face each other in pairs and to drum in turn, or, if using the tone bars, once on their own and once on their partner's tone bar. They can have great fun with this, developing it where their imagination leads them, drumming twice and then clicking sticks, or tapping each other (lightly!) on the head. It is not necessary for the teacher to request these playful variations, as they will happen naturally. They are beneficial, as they lead children to the awareness that they will only succeed if they watch each other closely, and are fully aware of each other's pulse and rhythm.

Then one child can learn a rhythmic phrase by watching the teacher drum it, and can then play it for a second child to copy. They can be asked to drum slowly or fast; then to execute a definite number of each. For example:

Then rests are introduced. For example:

Then a combination of all three. For example:

When the children are familiar with, and can play different combinations, they can be asked to divide into pairs, first playing simple crotchets together, and then alternately. They can then go on to share a sequence or phrase, for example:

the first child playing

and the second

This necessitates looking at each other and coordinating their playing, involving even more awareness of the other person, as well as of the overall phrase. By doing this, gradually a real feeling of pulse and rhythm is developed.

As the children's ability grows, more difficult tasks can be requested. For example, a "conversation" can be introduced: one child can play a rhythm, and another child answer with another different one. For example:

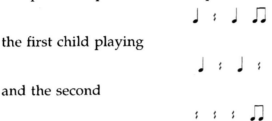

In a more difficult project, the teacher or one of the children beats the pulse, while another plays a different rhythm at the same time. Another child drumming a third rhythm can then be added.

As the pupils become more proficient, longer phrases can be attempted. Gradually a complex score can be developed, with each instrument playing a different rhythm. The understanding of music derived from this is "transferable"; it leads to an ability to construct more involved dance pieces, with each dancer dancing his or her own sequence while at the same time being part of the whole.

Dance Notation — Labanotation

Sometimes children who are deaf or hard of hearing find it difficult to see and copy a beaten rhythm, as fast beats can be too quick to be seen clearly and to count. In addition, the vibrations from one beat carry over onto the next and become blurred. This led me to the idea that as rhythm can not be heard, or only heard with difficulty, the introduction of a visual means of explaining it might be helpful, and I began to experiment with teaching dance notation.

I chose "Labanotation" (1977), as in this system the length of symbol coincides with the length of time it takes to execute a given movement. For example:

⊡ takes twice as long to execute as ⊡

I started by suggesting to children that each movement take an equal length of time. I then introduced the concept of moving in different directions by just using my hands to point forwards, backwards or sideways, and devised a game in which I pointed at random, and the children had to move in the same directions as those to which I pointed. Then my hands were replaced by cards depicting pointing hands; these were then changed to cards in which the drawings were shown alongside the relevant symbols, and finally the cards showed only the Labanotation symbols. At this stage symbols of varying lengths were notated in front of the children, and their relationship to the amount of time taken to execute them was discussed. From there it was a very small step to notating a simple dance on a sheet of paper, asking each child to work it out and to dance it. I was surprised at the speed with which this was accomplished by most of the children. As their skill and understanding progressed, it became possible to introduce high and low levels, floor patterns and dynamics.

As some dance teachers will know, Labanotation is written on a stave which is divided into bars and note values, often alongside a musical score. Some children had expressed a curiosity about the score. As I had begun increasingly to use percussion instruments and tone bars as an accompaniment for the dancing and to allow the children to use these, I started to teach music notation.

Music Notation

At first I did not believe that very young children could grasp the concept of "reading music", and I was very surprised to find that even those as young as three or four very quickly understood. The resemblance they saw between a drawing of a drumstick with its round head, and the symbol for a note of music seemed to facilitate this. They quickly learnt to beat simple rhythms using only four symbols:

♩   the Crotchet or $1/4$ note

♪   the Quaver or $1/8$ note, twice as fast as the crotchet

𝄽   the Rest, equivalent in length to the crotchet

-    under a note that is accented

Remarkably, I found that children began themselves to apply their new knowledge of music notation to their dance. For example, on one occasion I was working on a dance with some six-year-olds, and one of them was finding it hard to learn the sequence. Without being asked, a little girl dragged the one who was having problems to the board and wrote the rhythm down. After that there were no more difficulties.

Another time the children were learning a dance step with the rhythm

♩ 𝄽 ♩ 𝄽 ♩ ♩ ♩

and were having trouble executing it. They were then asked to clap it, and this helped in some cases. However, it was only when the sequence was written on the board that everyone suddenly understood and all problems disappeared.

The dotted rhythm is very common in many simple dance steps, for example the skip and the gallop:

♫♩.   ♫♩.

At first I hesitated to teach its notation, as musically it is a difficult concept to grasp. In the end, I did introduce it to nine- and ten-year-olds and later to even younger children. None of the children had any problem whatsoever with this dotted rhythm symbol, and simply accepted it and drummed correctly whenever they saw it. By writing quavers individually:

and the dotted rhythm thus:

the children find no difficulty in differentiating between the even rhythm and the dotted one. I do not attempt to explain why one is written one way and the other in another, or that the dot is equal to half again of the note it follows, until the children are able to understand the mathematical implications of this.

Both deaf and hearing children at times find difficulty in stringing musical phrases or bars together, often stopping at the end of each section before continuing with the next. It is as if they feel that the sight of the bar line gives them licence to stop and think before jumping over it to continue with the next bar. One way of overcoming this problem is to ask the children to bounce as they play, thus creating a pulse in their body. (Swaying is also possible, but seems to be harder). If this pulse is established, even young children can understand the concept of bar lines, finding no problem with bars of three or four beats, beating the rhythms, and also composing their own rhythms in their chosen tempo.

A useful game involving notation begins by asking a child to write a bar of music. The teacher should make sure that the child understands what he or she is writing. Then another student writes the next bar, building up to a sequence of about four bars. Another group writes another sequence, and then both groups beat their phrase at the same time, bouncing as they play. A composition by some eight-to-nine-year-olds was as follows:

Another way to increase understanding of bar lines is to introduce the idea of accents, as the first beat in every bar is often stressed or accented. However, accents can also be difficult for the deaf and hard of hearing to grasp, as the quieter sounds may not be heard and the contrast between accented notes and quiet notes hard to distinguish; when the profoundly deaf learn to talk, they often tend to speak in an even way, with no accented syllables. By combining notation with the request that the accented note be drummed with more energy than the others, the idea can successfully be transmitted. Once this is the case, the way lies open to explore music and dance in different meters, as for example $^3/_4$ or $^6/_8$.

I once taught a Spanish dance to a group of twelve-to-thirteen-year-olds. This was in three/four time, with the first beat of the bar accented:

The girls found it very difficult to dance and also to beat on the tambour. However when I next introduced the idea of accents to a group of six-to-seven-year-olds by notating it first, I found that the children had no problem whatsoever in understanding the idea or of emphasising the accented beat when drumming or dancing.

Music Making

Sometimes the more adventurous children, however deaf, may want to play a keyboard instrument, and he or she can be helped, (as can any child), by colour-coding the notes and matching the colours to the notation, until the sequences or tunes have been committed to memory. A couple of additional symbols can now be introduced as the keyboard is capable of playing longer notes:

- ♩, the Minim, or half-note, sustained for the length of two crotchets
- ω the Semibreve, or whole note, sustained for the length of four crotchets.

A profoundly deaf ten-year-old insisted on learning a tune by heart and, furthermore, on covering the keyboard so that he could not see the keys. He played perfectly, at the same time conducting several other children who were accompanying him on tone bars.

Tunes can be played on tone bars without the use of keyboards, each child playing his or her own bar, which is color-coordinated with the score. This is fun and is a useful exercise in developing awareness of each other.

A great deal of satisfaction can be derived by profoundly deaf children from the playing of a variety of instruments: strings, not only the bass or 'cello, but also the viola and even the violin; the guitar, whose vibrations are easy to feel as it is held close to the chest; and wind instruments also have been enjoyed by some children, to the surprise of their teachers.

The main difficulty when trying to play together is the problem of having to look at each other while looking at the score *and* at their instruments. Gradually the children learn to beat or play without looking at the instrument, and can learn to memorize simple rhythms so that they do not need to look at the notation. It is then possible to look at the child who is conducting, and who can emphasise the pulse by bending the knees on each beat. He or she can nod the head on the first beat off every bar, which is accented. Alternatively, the score can be projected, while the "conductor" points at each note. The problems are lessened when dancing, as it is easier to feel and to see each other's rhythms.

I have talked about this work to music teachers who have been surprised that these tasks can be accomplished by profoundly deaf children, and perhaps it has been a case of "Fools rush in where angels fear to tread".* But I have found that as long as this rhythm work is visual, is notated, and is not only drummed but also danced and experienced with the whole body, the children gradually develop the ability to cope with quite complex rhythms and sequences leading to complete musical phrases, with really exciting results.

A good way to familiarize the children with playing and to enhance their confidence in doing so is to choose a simple song which they know, such as "Happy Birthday". Notate the rhythm on the board and add the words underneath. All the children can play together in unison, if enough instruments are available. Alternatively each child can be given a tone bar marked with a different colour. The familiar melody can be notated using corresponding coloured notes, and can then be "read" as the children play only the notes which match their instrument's colour. To aid memory, tone bars on which eighth notes (quavers) are played can be placed at right angles to those on which quarter notes (crotchets) are played. Whichever method is used to involve all the children in playing the tune, great fun will be had by all.

Signed singing has became very popular on both sides of the Atlantic, and this can be great fun and of much benefit if a definite pulse is established. This can easily be done by swaying before the signing commences, and maintaining this movement as a basis on which to build. In this way, the signing too will develop a rhythm of it own, echoing that of the sung words. By establishing this very physical way of signing, the "muscle memory" can take over, making it less important and finally unnecessary for a hearing person to lead the activity. The strong body movements can also facilitate the production of vocal sounds — but that is not within the scope of this book.

Signed singing, along with rhythmic warm-up exercises, simple folk dances, clapping, drumming, the use of music and dance notation, and other instrumental music-making, all help to awaken the "inner rhythm" — the vital ingredient for turning rhythm into dance.

---

* However, Paul Gouge has been doing pioneering work in England in the area of teaching music to the deaf; see his forthcoming book to be published by Harwood Academic Press.

6

RHYTHM INTO DANCE

Combining music-making with dancing nurtures the growth of children's "inner rhythm". It enriches the teacher's efforts to help children feel pulse, meter, rhythm and rhythmic phrasing through large rhythmical movements of the body. The direct, physical experience of rhythmic playing aids the deaf children's conscious understanding of the relationship between rhythm and dance.

Just how powerful this can be in helping children make the connection between rhythm and dance is illustrated by an early discovery I made while teaching. I had often had difficulty in communicating to deaf children the idea that *dance has a rhythm of its own*, and is not something totally divorced from drumming or music. The children would sit and correctly clap or beat a rhythm, but when asked to dance the same rhythm, they did not understand how to do so.

It was not until I suggested that they pretend that the floor was a giant drum which they could beat with their feet that they understood! The image of the *floor as a drum*, combined with their physical experience of *beating a drum* made it easy for them first to beat the rhythm with their feet while sitting, and then to stand up and dance the rhythm with accuracy.

Tap dancing is a technique which develops this idea. It is easy to learn and is greatly enjoyed by children of all ages. The feet execute the rhythms which can become complex as ability increases.

Drumming and Dancing — Activity Ideas

Themes

All of the themes discussed in Chapter 4 can provide a rich resource for drumming and dancing activities. For example, the "Animals" theme is always popular with young children. One can begin with a discussion of the ways in which different animals move: whether slowly or fast, heavily or lightly, evenly or jerkily and so on. Children can then be asked to drum accordingly.

A dance element can then be added. One child can be asked to chose an animal, then to beat the drum while the teacher mimes the animal's movement: the slow, heavy plod of the elephant, the smooth prowl of the tiger, the gallop of a horse, the fast jump of a rabbit, the sudden stops of any animal as it freezes in fear. Gradually, it is possible to introduce a regular dance-beat — for example, three walks and "freeze", or three walks and "eat very fast" — while the children drum the rhythm of three beats and "rest" at the same speed.

With older children, pairs or groups of children can drum while other pairs or groups are dancing. The "Weather" theme offers many varying tempi, rhythms, and images (rain, storm, snow, lightning, sunshine) for dance accompanied by drumming. "Emotions" is also an effective theme: dancers can convey emotion by stamping angrily, creeping fearfully, slowly and sadly dragging the feet, or skipping happily while another group drums.

Conducting — Drummers may watch dancers directly as they accompany, or children may take it in turn to initiate the drumming, acting as conductor. Drummers become quite adept at watching a "Conductor" (Plate 7), and children who conduct soon become skilful at conducting fast or slowly, with stressed notes or long phrases.

Which? Game — A guessing game can be played — "Which Animal?" or "Which Feeling?" or "Which kind of Weather?", in which children have to listen to or watch the drumstick and dance the answer.

Another variation of this game is to play it without a definite question or theme: children simply dance as they watch or listen. When the drumming stops, they also must do so; they are then asked to watch for changes in tempo; pauses are then introduced, then accented and weak beats, and finally definite rhythms are played. Children are able to improvise dance according to the rhythm they see, hear or feel.

Some schools are very keen to develop the residual hearing of the children and these games and those outlined below can be played without the children seeing the drum but rather having to listen. Alternatively in a mixed class, emphasis can be put on watching as this is such an important skill for the deaf and hard of hearing. Those who can hear the drumbeat will do so anyway, and will dare to turn away as they dance.

Watch! Game

Understanding can be greatly enhanced if the children are allowed to play drums or other instruments for each other, which they love to do, as they then become physically aware of the various possibilities. This can be turned into a game, with the last one to stop or the one who did not follow the rhythm being "out" and having to sit and watch. The watching is again useful, as the children can see the consequences of not paying attention to the drumstick.

Drum and Dance Relay

Another game for very young children can be to ask them to run to the drum a little way away, beat a given rhythm and then dance the same rhythm, and then to run back and to hand the drumstick to another child. Their imagination and creativity can then be brought into play by asking one child to devise a rhythm, play it and dance it.

Rhythms into Dance

Dancing a Rhythmic Sequence

The next stage will be to set a longer sequence, and to make sure that all children know it and can beat or clap it. This can be done by first asking one of them to notate it on the board. The children are then asked to work in pairs, devising different way of dancing to the notated rhythm. This greatly enhances their sociability as well as their determination to get it right, for it is very difficult to dance with a partner who is bouncing up and down at different times! (Plate 8, 9).

At first it may be necessary to suggest and demonstrate a movement vocabulary for the children, proposing that they move their heads, shoulders, torsos, and arms, that they can jump travel and turn. They soon do not need these ideas and will create wonderfully imaginative dances of their own. It is often a good idea to set aside a few moments for the children to show what they have done, giving them an opportunity for pride, as well as developing their critical faculties as they look at and evaluate the efforts of others. Sometimes the children find it difficult to remember a rhythm, and I find it very exciting to see them looking over their shoulder at the board as they refresh their memory by reading the score.

This task can be turned into a game: the children stand in a circle, and one skips round inside stopping in front of another child. The one in the centre then dances a sequence to a given rhythm, the other has to copy it, and they dance it together; it is now the second child's turn to skip round. The other children can clap the accompaniment as this game is played.

Alternatively, the children divide into pairs, and one can drum a rhythm while the other must dance it, taking it in turns to drum and dance. This process can be reversed: one child dances a sequence and the partner tries to drum or clap the same rhythm (Plates 10, 11, 12).

This exercise can be given to students of varying ages and degrees of ability as long as the pairs are well matched, as their dance will tend to reflect their understanding of the rhythm they have chosen. Older ones can devise longer rhythmic sequences or may prefer a more modern dance as for example rock 'n roll, described in the chapter on themes. They can learn to beat the rhythm:

$$\quad \flat \quad \flat \quad \flat \quad \flat \;\vdots\; \flat \quad \flat \quad \flat \quad \flat \;\flat$$

and can learn the appropriate footwork and style from videos of old films if the teacher does not feel confident enough to teach them, and can then accompany each other.

Conversations and Duets

As their ability increases, they can devise conversations where the drummers creates a rhythm which is answered by a different one by the dancer. They can then execute a duet where the rhythm of the drummer is complemented by that of the dancer. Eventually they can be encouraged to compose and dance in meters other than $4/4$. For example, while it is not difficult to sit and drum in $3/4$, it can cause problems when dancing, as it often necessitates initiating movements with alternate feet and this is something which the untrained dancer can at first find hard.

Drum and Dance into Dance

Dance and drumming can be used together when creating a dance. For example, I showed a class of profoundly deaf eight-year-olds some of whom had additional learning difficulties, a video of professional dancers performing a Ghanaian Harvest Dance. In this dance the natural actions of preparing the ground, planting and harvesting are clearly if stylistically portrayed. We then sat and discussed the different activities necessary for the growing of crops: clearing a space in the jungle, hoeing and breaking up the ground, planting the seeds, watching the plants grow, harvesting, shaking the chaff off the feet, and finally dancing to celebrate the successful harvest. The children then mimed these movements, gradually enlarging them until an even pulse emerged. As each activity was enacted, every child accompanied the others on the drum, evolving suitable and sometimes very innovative and interesting rhythms. The dance was finally performed for the school in clothes which the children themselves had tie-dyed, with each child taking it in turn to play for a different activity.

Work activities of our society are often also a good starting point for rhythmic dancing and drumming together: digging, sawing, hammering, chopping, sweeping, dusting, window cleaning, the possibilities are endless. Start with the activity, enlarge the movements, and then get other children to drum the accompaniment, echoing the tempo, dynamics, rhythm and pauses as they watch.

For very young children, the actions can be strung together to tell a simple story. For slightly older ones an activity can be made into a dance sequence as for example when cutting down a tree: three chops and wipe the sweat off the brow, or three bangs on the hammer and hold an aching back. For more mature pupils, the activity can be used as a starting point, stylised so much that it becomes virtually unrecognizable as they explore the qualities of the movement when dancing in different directions or levels, in varying relationships with each other. The shape or dynamics of the movement can be replicated in various ways as the students execute, for example the circular movement of the woodcutter, coming down heavily and circling quickly away to descend heavily again, after a slight suspension at the height of the circle. This repetitive circular movement can be done in different directions and on different levels, extended until the whole body is involved, in jumping or travelling, in relation to colleagues, at the same time or in sequence, standing in line, or in circles creating ever changing floor patterns.

These can all be incorporated into a group dance, employing varying timings and musical devices such as fugues, with the pupils taking it in turn to initiate a sequence. There are so many possibilities.

The Dancer as Musician

These different activities of dancing and drumming culminate when the dancer accompanies him or herself by an instrument which is held and played while dancing. For example, a tarantella is usually performed with a tambourine which the dancer shakes or beats in time with his or her own dancing, and there are dances in many parts of the world in which in which the dancers clap, or hold a drum or cymbals. The beating of the instrument is an integral part of the choreography. This idea can be adapted according to the instruments available and to which the children can respond. If live accompaniment is used it may be possible to feel its vibrations through the instrument which is being held.

The children can be asked to sway from side to side with both arms stretched out, one hand holding a tambourine. Then one arm makes a semi-circle over the head to beat the tambourine, and sweeps back on the same path. Simple footwork can be added, for example: step close, step close; or a complementary one can be attempted such as: step close to the left as the tambourine is beaten with the right hand, and three fast steps to the right as the working arm swings back again. The tambourine can be hit while skipping, in front of the body on the first skip, and behind it while leaning forward on the second. This can be done turning, or travelling forwards, backwards or sideways. Once they understand the principle, the children themselves can create many wonderful dance sequences which, furthermore, they will almost certainly execute in a thoroughly rhythmical way (Plates 13, 14, 15).

7

INNER RHYTHM FOR *ALL*

The methods described in the preceding chapters were originally developed in Special schools for profoundly deaf children. As a result of their training in Inner Rhythm, many of the pupils improved in their ability to dance, and they were eventually able to take their place in regular dance classes alongside their hearing friends. They no longer needed continuous specific attention to rhythm, dynamics and phrasing.

These same techniques were then employed when teaching partially deaf children in units in mainstream schools. Here they also were of benefit, though a slightly different emphasis was found to be necessary. For example, these children were often faster in picking up a drummed rhythm, as they were more accustomed to having to use their residual hearing to communicate with their mainstream teachers and hearing classmates. And of course many had more hearing than most of the children in Special schools. As a result their need to read music notation was not as great, and they often did not do this as well as the profoundly deaf children.

Hearing children and others who had been encouraged to use their voices often found it easier, initially, to breathe deeply. As I worked with them alongside profoundly deaf and partially hearing children, it became clear to me just how important deep breathing is for *all* children in the development of both strong rhythmic movements and — even more critical to the growth of "inner rhythm" — an inner understanding of the breath and phrasing inherent in dance.

Deaf children who have undergone Inner Rhythm training have at times appeared to be more musical than their hearing peers who have not. They know that they have to *pay attention to the accompaniment*, whether by listening, watching or feeling the vibrations. Hearing children, accustomed as they often are to modern pop music with its insistent beat, rarely listen carefully to the music, and do not hear the subtleties of dynamics and phrasing.

In an integrated class of deaf and hearing children, care must be taken to boost the confidence of the deaf, and to give special help where necessary with breathing, body awareness, use of space and relation to others while imparting these skills to the whole class. Once these have been acquired, the child who is deaf or hard of hearing will have no problem in following the lesson with his or her hearing peers.

Deaf children may at times also appear to start off with less technical ability, but this is due mainly to the fact that they lack confidence and also need special help with the understanding of rhythm. Usually, after some Inner Rhythm training, the technical competence of *all* will improve, and differences in ability will disappear as they realize that when learning to execute a difficult step the first task is to acquaint themselves with its rhythm. Relevant to this is the observation made by Chris de Marigny (1992), after she watched hearing dance students participating in a workshop in African dance at the Laban centre. She noticed that the insistence on rhythm allowed the student to pick up and memorize steps at greater speed than normal, and she surmised that this put the memory in the muscles themselves, enabling the dancers to experience the totality of the phrase long before they had mastered the technique.

Movement skills of all children can also be enhanced by an approach focusing on inner rhythm; as children acquire the ability to listen, they learn how accented notes can be danced strongly, thus giving impetus to execute a high jump or a fast movement. They can discover that by breathing in as the music soars and exhaling as it descends, they can use the music to help them to sustain a position or to make a slow movement. As they learn to listen they can also react to the mood of the music, to its excitement or its stillness.

They can all also benefit from "seeing" music, approaching an understanding of it through visual means. The teaching of the basics of music notation takes very little time and can be taught to all students, eventually going far beyond the fundamentals. As the pupils' understanding of rhythm increases, they can be introduced to the varying sounds of different instruments, and also to high and low pitch. The deaf can learn to feel these differences, whereas the hearing students will of course be able to hear them. They can all learn to read scores where two or more instruments enter and stop at different times and execute varying rhythms, and they can accompany each other from existing scores, as well as composing specially devised pieces. As a result their understanding of choreography both as dancers and as creators will be enhanced. Alternatively, dance notation can acquaint the children not only with musical values but also with qualities, directions, levels, relationships, the very language of dance itself.

By learning to dance in silence, by becoming aware of Inner Rhythm, children learn to think about and explore movement, to become aware of its own pulse, meter, rhythm and breath. By learning to create movement sequences with attention to music — its tempi, meters, dynamics, melodic movements and moods — young people enrich their dance ability and creativity. They learn to hear with their bodies. Inner Rhythm can be for everyone.

BIBLIOGRAPHY

Aesop (1993) *The Best of Aesop's Fables,* London: Walker Books, first published 1990

Jacques-Dalcroze, E. (1992) *Rhythm, Music and Education.* The Dalcroze Society

Dutoit, C.L. (1965) *Music Movement Therapy.* London, B.M. Dalcroze

Ellwood, J. & Webster, A. (1985) *The Hearing Impaired Child in the Ordinary School.* Beckenham: Croom Helm Ltd.

Griffiths, A., Howarth, I., Wood, D., Wood, H., (1987) *Teaching and Talking With Deaf Children.* Chichester: John Wiley and Sons

Hutchinson, A. (1977) 1954, 1970, *Labanotation, The system of Analyzing and Recording Movement,* New York: Theatre Arts Books

Kyle, J. (1987) ed. *Sign and School.* Clevedon, Philadelphia: Multilingual Matters

de Marigny, C. (1992) New African Dance in *Dance Theatre Journal* Volume 9, No. 3, Spring 1992, pp. 4–7. London: Laban Centre

Moore, B.C., (1991) *An Introduction to the Psychology of Hearing.* Sidcup: Academic Press

Pickles, J.O., (1988) *An Introduction to the Physiology of Hearing.* Sidcup: Academic Press

Three Little Pigs (1978). Loughborough: Ladybird Books

Rambert, M. (1972) *Quicksilver.* London, Basingstoke: Macmillan London Ltd.

Ross, M. (1983) *The Arts: A Way of Knowing.* Oxford: Pergamon Press

Sacks, O. (1989) *Seeing Voices.* Berkeley and Los Angeles: University of California Press. (1990) London: Pan Books

Sherlock, P. (retold by), (1990), *West Indian Folk-Tales.* Oxford: Oxford University Press, first published 1966

Witkin, (1974) *The Intelligence of Feeling.* London: Heinemann Educational Books

Wood, D. (1988) 1989, 1990 *How Children Think and Learn.* Oxford: Basil Blackwell Ltd

Film

Anderson, H. and Medoff, M. (1986) (after screenplay by Medoff, M.) *Children of a Lesser God.* Paramount Pictures

APPENDIX

Musical Instruments I Have Found Most Useful

All the instruments are Sonor Percussion Instruments, and can be obtained from:

MUSIC EDUCATION SUPPLIES LTD
101 Bansted Road South
Sutton
Surrey
SM2 5LH
U.K.   tel: 0181 770 3866

Music Education Supplies have a very wide variety of instruments. Below is a list of those which I have found most useful. I suggest that teachers starting off in the field obtain a catalogue, and experiment with a few instruments, before buying large numbers.

Beaters (Mallets)	
Sch 7	felt-headed, large head, for hand drums and hanging cymbals
Sch 8	wool-felt, for Deep Bass and Contra-Bass Chime or tone bars
Chime, or Tone Bars	Rosewood with individual resonators made of wood. All sizes, although most children prefer large ones with the lower frequencies
Hanging cymbals	V 2003, 13-inch diameter, silver-bronze
Kettledrums.	Acrylic, easily transportable. These are supplied in 4 sizes. I prefer the largest: 29-inch P290 range approximately C – A

Palisono Xylophones made of fibreglass.   These come in a variety of sizes and frequencies

Tambour or Hand drum	V 1624, 20-inch diameter, genuine calfskin or goatskin

Tambourine	V 1637, 10-inch diameter. These come in smaller sizes, which makes them easier to handle while dancing, but harder for many children to hear.
Triangles	V 2355, 9½-inch, silver steel alloy

Recordings I Have Found Useful

Pop music of today
Pop music of yesterday: Charleston, Tango, Rock 'n' Roll, Twist, etc.
Scott Joplin
Circus Music
Folk music from:
    Brazil
    Ghana
    India
    Israel
    Russia
    Sri Lanka
    West Indies
Waltzes
Polkas
Tomita's electronic performance of Debussy's *Golliwog's Cakewalk*

Specific themes

Work actions:
"Hey Ho, Hey Ho, It's off to Work We Go" from Walt Disney's *Snow White*

Space:
Tomita's electronic performance of Debussy's *Footprints in the Snow*

Underwater:
Tomita's electronic performance of Debussy's *Claire de Lune*, and *Engulfed Cathedral*

Witches, Wizards:
Grieg's *In the Hall of the Mountain King*

Animals:
Saint Saen's *Carnival of the Animals*

Useful Addresses in the U.K.

BEETHOVEN FUND FOR DEAF CHILDREN
2 Queensmead
St. John's Wood Park
London NW8 6RE   tel: 0171 586 8107

LONDON DISABILITY ARTS FORUM
34 Osnaburgh Street
London N1 3ND   tel: 0171 916 5419

ROYAL NATIONAL INSTITUTE FOR THE DEAF
105 Gower Street
London WC1E 6AH   tel: 0171 387 8033

THE NATIONAL DEAF CHILDREN'S SOCIETY
15 Dufferin Street
London EC14 8PD   tel: 0171 250 0123

Organisations teaching or performing in the area of dance and deafness

COMMON GROUND SIGN DANCE THEATRE
Hanwell Community Centre
Westcott Crescent
London W7 IPD   tel: 0181 575 1078

CONTEMPORARY DANCE TRUST
The Place
17 Duke's Road
London WC1H 9AB   tel: 0171 388 8956

DANCE FOR EVERYONE
6 Milverton Road
London NW6 7AS   tel: 0181 451 2000

GRAEAE THEATRE COMPANY
24 Bayham Street
London NW1 OEY   tel: 0171 383 7541

FESTIVAL OF PERFORMING ARTS
National Deaf Children's Society
24 Wakefield Road
Rothwell Haigh
Leeds LS26 OSF   tel: 053 282 3458

LONDON DISABILITY ARTS FORUM
Diorama Arts Centre
34 Osnaburgh Street
London NW1 3ND   tel: 0171 916 5419

SHAPE LONDON
Deaf Arts Section
1 Thorpe Close
London W10 5XL   tel: 0181 960 9245

THE BASIC THEATRE COMPANY
33 Blegbrough Road
London SQ16 6DL   tel: 0181 871 3846

THEATRE OF THE DEAF
University of Reading
Department of Arts and Humanities
Bulmershe Court
Early
Reading RG6 1HY   tel: 0734 875 123

THEATRE VENTURE
Top Floor
3 Mills School
Abbey Lane
Stratford
London E15 2RP   tel: 0181 519 6678

UNICORN THEATRE
Great Newport Street
London WC2H 7JB   tel: 0171 379 3280

Dance in the National Curriculum (U.K.)

Dance forms part of *Physical Education in the National Curriculum*. It was prepared by the Secretaries of State for Education and Science and for Wales, and was published by Her Majesty's Stationery office (HMSO) in April 1992.

The National Curriculum outlines attainment targets and programmes of study for four key stages of a child's development in each subject: Key Stage 1 deals with education up to the age of seven; Key Stage 2, up to eleven; Key Stage 3, up to 14; and Key Stage 4, up to 16.

In their rationale for physical education, the authors claim that "of all the activities in physical education, only dance, as an art form in its own right, is characterised by the intention and ability to make symbolic statements to create meaning. This ... distinguishes dance from other physical activities, and shares characteristics with music, drama and art. These art forms are the basis for children's artistic education."

In spite of this claim, dance is only compulsory up to the age of eleven. After that, it is optional.

By the end of Key Stage 1, children are expected to have experienced and developed control and coordination; to have explored contrasts of, for example, speed, direction, and level, and to describe what they have done. They should have experienced working with a range of stimuli, including music, and have been helped to develop rhythmic responses. This is the only area which would need to be modified when working with deaf children. Most students would not react automatically to different kinds of musical stimulus. Some might have to be helped to appreciate differences by feeling vibrations and by using residual hearing. For others this may be too difficult. But all can benefit from increased attention to rhythm. All children should have been given opportunities to explore moods and feelings. Finally, they should have started to make dances.

At the end of Key Stage 2, children are expected to be able to make dances, involving improvising, sometimes incorporating work from other aspects of the curriculum, in particular music, art and drama. They should be given the opportunity to increase their range of bodily movements, and to be guided to enrich these by varying shape, size, direction, speed and tension. They should be able to create simple characters and narratives in movement.

By the end of Key Stage 3, the children are expected to have refined and developed all the skills outlined above, and to have been taught how to use appropriate methods of composition, styles of accompaniment and techniques, when creating and performing their own dances. They should show an understanding of dance style, and be able to describe and analyse dances in relation to aspects of production and cultural contexts.

Finally, by the end of Key Stage 4, all aspects of their training will have developed still further, and the students will have been given the opportunity to dance in a range of styles. They will have been given opportunities to create dances which communicate artistic intention, and they will be able to record the process of composition. They will be given opportunities to describe and evaluate all aspects of dance including choreography, performance, cultural and historical contexts and production.

Contents of the video, which can be purchased to accompany this book.

The video is designed to show the process of development of Inner Rhythm in profoundly deaf children.

The author would like to thank all staff members from Blanche Nevile, Grove House, Hacton, Hawkswood and Heathlands Schools for their co-operation and assistance in the production of this video. Very many thanks are due also to the children for their participation.

INDEX

Lightning Source UK Ltd.
Milton Keynes UK
03 February 2011

166821UK00001B/72/A